New Light on the
History of the
Taiping Rebellion

New Light on the History of the Taiping Rebellion

By

Ssu-yü Teng

Professor of History, Indiana University

NEW YORK / RUSSELL & RUSSELL
1966

PREFACE

The rise of Chinese Communism to power makes it more than ever essential that the West understand the historical origin and nature of the revolutionary process in China. The great Taiping Rebellion of a century ago has long been recognized both in China and the West as the significant opening phase of this process.

The present work by Dr. Teng Ssu-yü is a bibliographical survey of the modern historical studies which have been made in China and elsewhere on the subject of the Taipings. This survey is offered as an interim report on what is being done in a very lively field of historical investigation. It is put out in this form under the auspices of the International Secretariat of the Institute of Pacific Relations, with the thought that it may facilitate the work of Western scholars in this important field. No similarly comprehensive survey of the recent literature on the Taiping Rebellion is available elsewhere.

The most fundamental research on the whole range of problems connected with the Rebellion has been under way for several years at the Far Eastern Institute of the University of Washington, under the direction of Professor George Taylor, whose article of 1933, "The Taiping Rebellion, Its Economic Background and Social Theory," (The Chinese Social and Political Science Review, vol. 16), marked the beginning of a new analytic interest in the Taipings on the part of Western social scientists. Research monographs of the group of scholars working under Professors Taylor, Michael, Wilhelm, and others at the University of Washington will soon appear and will inaugurate a new phase in our understanding of the whole subject.

Meanwhile, the present survey of materials and publications in the field of Taiping studies will be of timely and widespread interest to the increasing number of Western students of Modern China, at centers in the United States and elsewhere. Dr. Teng is well known in the field of Chinese studies for his bibliographical and other publications. In this survey he presents brief summaries of the work produced by leading Chinese scholars and by writers outside of China, and analyzes their treatment of several fascinating historical problems. His survey of the causes, phases, and other aspects of the Rebellion reflects the pioneer work of these scholars in recent years and indicates the extent of present knowledge and opinion; naturally it does not pretend to accomplish in a brief essay that fundamental analysis of the traditional Chinese society and its complex processes which may be expected in forthcoming studies of broader scope.

John K. Fairbank

Cambridge, Mass.
December 1949

CONTENTS

NEW LIGHT ON THE HISTORY OF THE TAIPING REBELLION

Introduction

The Taiping rebellion (1851-1864)[1] has attracted much interest
during the last few decades, and many Western and Chinese scholars
are making special studies of it. Although many branches of Chinese
art and literature have been degenerating during the recent long
years of deplorable war, historical research has made considerable
progress,[2] especially in the study of the Taiping rebellion or revolution.[3] This movement occupies a key position for the understanding
of China in the twentieth century, and because of its significance,
it may be of some use to present a critical summary of the new light
which has been thrown on Taiping history, in which I have maintained
a continued interest after having composed in 1937-38 most of the
biographies of both government and rebel leaders of the period in the
Eminent Chinese of the Ch'ing Period, edited by Arthur W. Hummel.
The material for this study is taken mainly from Chinese sources
published during the last fifteen or twenty years and is for the
benefit of those who do not have access to these volumes. It is, however, not a mere bibliographical essay, nor a bare summary, but an
analysis of the old and new materials with personal ideas expressed
under various headings.

I. HISTORY OF THE STUDY OF THE TAIPING REBELLION

The treatment of the Taiping movement has undergone several
stages. The first stage, which occurred shortly after the failure of
the movement, was characterized by a contempt for the insurgents and
by the destruction or censorship of historical relics and documents
such as Tseng Kuo-fan's treatment of Li Hsiu-ch'eng's confession or
written statement made in jail.

The second stage was one of blind praise of the rebel cause as
an encouragement to Dr. Sun Yat-sen's revolutionary movement against
the Manchu regime. At the beginning of Sun's revolutionary adventure

Sun's nickname was Hung Hsiu-ch'üan, because he was very familiar with
the stories of the Taipings. Based on this historical and psychological
background, Sun's adherents utilized the Taiping history to do propaganda work. One of the earliest of such publications is Huang Shih-chung's
Hung Hsiu-ch'üan yen-i, a novel imitating the style of the Romance of the
Three Kingdoms published in Canton in 1908, but it is criticized as inaccurate and incomplete both in its collection of material and in its
scope (fifty-four chapters ending at the surrender of Li Chao-shou in
1858).[4] In 1923 the Unofficial History of the Taiping T'ien-kuo by
Ling Shan-ch'ing was published, in which the author gives a fairly
detailed description of the Taiping official and military systems, and
a good discussion of the causes of its rise and fall. The book is
sympathetic to the Taipings, though the material is based on official
sources of the Manchu government.[5]

The third stage was the discovery of the books issued by the
Taipings, preserved in the libraries of foreign countries. The discovery was first made by a few Japanese scholars,[6] and later Chinese
students in Paris, London, and Berlin copied in part or in whole more
than ten Taiping documents and had them published in China. The first
publication of such material was Ch'en Yen-sheng's T'ai-p'ing T'ien-kuo
shih-liao ti-i-chi in 1925, consisting of ten official documents of the
rebels.[7] In the following year, a publisher issued Liu Fu's T'ai-p'ing
T'ien-kuo yu-ch'ü wen-chien shih-liu chung,[8] which copies sixteen
"interesting" documents. Liu's criterion of selecting material by its
interesting nature kept him from copying that which had real historical
value. Those primary sources, reintroduced to China, though fragmentary,
gave Chinese scholars a great stimulus to search for more information
in all lands. Thus a very important source soon appeared, Tsei-ch'ing
hui-tsuan (A Classified compilation of the Rebel's Information, 12 chüan)
compiled by Chang Tê-chien under the auspices of Tseng Kuo-fan (1811-1872)
and published as late as 1932 in facsimile from a rare manuscript in the
Sinological Library of Nanking.

As a result of these books there came the fourth state of Taiping
studies led by Hsieh Hsing-yao, Chien Yu-wen and others who hunted for
still more new materials from all possible sources. Hsieh has carefully

studied many individual records of the contemporaries of the rebels and Chien is famous for his field investigations of the revolutionary spots and his use of English sources.

In 1936 Hsiao I-shan compiled the T'ai-p'ing T'ien-kuo ts'ung-shu or the Taiping Documents Series in which twenty-three works are reproduced in facsimile mostly from the collection of the British Museum.[9] Hsiao also compiled the Taiping decrees and correspondence published by the Peiping Research Institute in 1935 entitled T'ai-p'ing T'ien-kuo chao-yü consisting of twenty-one documents. Wang Chung-min, an expert on bibliography who worked in the Bibliotheque Nationale and the Library of Congress for many years, also compiled the T'ai-p'ing T'ien-kuo kuan-shu pu-pien[10] containing ten titles, although they have not been completely published. Yü Ta-wei copied some material from the Berlin Library and this was compiled by Lo Yung and Shen Tsu-chi into T'ai-p'ing T'ien-kuo shih-wen ch'ao published by the Commercial Press in 1934. In addition, the Wen-hsien ts'ung-pien, Chang-ku ts'ung-pien and the Ch'ing shih-lu make available most of the official source materials on the Taiping.

Since the appearance of these important collections and further publication of sources[11] in I-ching, Ta-feng and other magazines, there are only seven Taiping official publications which are still unavailable.[12]

The scholars of Taiping history are passing from the stage of hunting for material to that of critical study, digestion, interpretation, and rewriting of the whole history, and thus are creating the present stage in the pursuit of Taiping history which is headed toward a scientific interpretation and an overall treatment of the whole period. There are many experts working toward this goal, and their achievements are noteworthy, but the time is still far off for any individual to produce a monumental, complete history of this period.

II. A GENERAL REVIEW OF THE WORKS OF THE TAIPING HISTORIANS

1. Chien Yu-wen

Among the present day Taiping historians whose chief interest and energy have been devoted to this period for many years, we may first review the work of Chien Yu-wen who has so far published three volumes:

T'ai-p'ing T'ien-kuo tsa-chi (Miscellaneous Notes about the Heavenly Kingdom of Great Peace, 1935), Chin-t'ien chih-yu chi chi-t'a (A Trip to Chin-t'ien and Other Essays, 1944), and T'ai-p'ing chün Kwang-hsi shou-i shih (A History of the Beginning of the Revolution of the Taiping Army in Kwangsi, 1944). All these books were published by the Commercial Press and many chapters in these volumes were previously contributed as essays to periodicals, such as I-ching, Ta-feng, and others. Chien was a Cantonese who received his A.B. degree from Oberlin College and M.A. degree from the University of Chicago. In the latter institution he had further training in theology and collected material on Taiping Christianity for his Ph.D. dissertation. However, because of his mother's illness he had to give up his plans for a degree and return home.[1] His training enabled him to make wide use of both English and Chinese sources, the Taiping historical objects and the accounts of many foreign observers in China. He may be considered a field worker of Taiping history and a sympathetic expositor of the movement. His accurate and readable translations into Chinese of many articles or treatises from old English newspapers, magazines, or rare books make a very valuable contribution to the history of the period in China.

In the first volume, the Miscellaneous Notes about the Taiping T'ien-kuo, he has translated into Chinese The Visions of Hung-Siu-tshuen and Origin of the Kwang-Si Insurrection by Theodore Hamberg. In 1935 the work, which previously was not available in many libraries, was also reproduced with the English version in a separate volume by Yenching University under the title, T'ai-p'ing T'ien-kuo ch'i-i chi. The second entry in Chien's book is a translation of the Reverend M.T. Yates' lecture on "The Taiping Rebellion." The third is G.L. Wolseley's Narrative of the War with China, Chapter XIV, and the fourth and the fifth are also translations. It is a surprise to find that even a modern-trained scholar like Chien Yu-wen does not give full bibliographical data of the sources from which the translations were made. Other articles about the Taiping coins, literature, and the historical poems are also useful, but the most important one is concerned with the inquiries about the descendants of the Hung family. It has first-hand

information by which many previous speculations about Hung's real name
and family background are proved wrong.

Chien's second work, A Trip to Chin-t'ien and Other Essays, is based
mainly on his personal investigations in several historical spots of the
Taipings and his discovery of biographical material on Shih Ta-k'ai,
Hung Tê-ch'üan, and other leaders. The last entry is a review of the
rise and fall of the Heavenly Kingdom of Great Peace in which he expresses
his ideas about the whole movement. Although Chien has made some contribution in this work, his observation, that the treaties of Tientsen
(1858) and Peking (1860) were signed on the condition that the Western
Powers would help the Manchus to suppress the rebellion (p. 219) lacks
documentary evidence.

The third book, A History of the Beginning of the Revolution of
the Taiping Army in Kwangsi, is an attempt to write out the early part
of the history of the Taiping revolution based on the other two books.
This book was first published in magazines and after being revised six
times it is in the present form. The work is carefully done and has
made many authoritative conclusions. Although Chien has thus far spent
most of his time on the first part of the revolution, he plans to write
an impressive volume for the whole period of Taiping history.

2. Hsieh Hsing-yao

Another Taiping historian is Hsieh Hsing-yao, a graduate of
Peking University, whose main publication is the T'ai-p'ing T'ien-kuo
shih-shih lun-tsung (Miscellaneous Discussions of the Historical Events
of the Taiping T'ien-kuo) published in 1935 by the Commercial Press.
It contains twelve articles written from 1924 to 1934. The best seems
to be the sixth article, "The Death of the Loyal Prince, Li Hsiu-ch'eng,
and Doubts on His Written Statements." The eleventh article, "The Brief
Facts about Li Chao-shou" is also well written, and the fifth entry,
"The Biography of Ch'ien Chiang" though not without mistakes, is a
collection of much valuable material. His ideas in the third essay are
out of date, and the last essay, dealing with the international relations of the Kingdom of Great Peace, is the weakest.

The second work of Hsieh Hsing-yao is T'ai-p'ing T'ien-kuo ts'ung-shu

shih-san chung (A Collectanea of Thirteen Taiping Documents) published
in 1938 by the compiler himself. This so-called collectanea is divided
into three parts, each of which makes a volume (t'se). The first part
consists of well written articles, postfaces, anecdotes, and desultory
notes about the Taipings. The first five essays trace the early history
of the revolution from its commencement to the sad end of the northern
expedition. Among these pages the mistake of reproducing Hung Ta-ch'üan'
picture as Hung Hsiu-ch'üan's is pointed out.[2] There is also a good
description of Li Hung-chang's headache over the arrogant and expensive
"Ever-Victorious Army" which was not only hard to control, but also unreliable because it frequently sold munitions and had secret connections
with the enemy (p. 42). The desultory notes also present much valuable
material such as the anecdotes of the Taiping kings, the problem as to
whether or not their land system was put into practice, the degree of
thoroughness of prohibition against opium and tobacco, the destruction
of cultural objects, and so on.

The second part of the T'ai-p'ing T'ien-kuo ts'ung-shu is a repro-
duction of seven rare books or manuscripts, namely: the Chin-ling kuei-
chia chi-shih lüeh (A Brief Record of the Events at Nanking in 1853
and 1854)[3] by Hsieh Chia-ho, who was a captive in the capital and later
put down on paper what he recalled having seen and heard there; the
Yüeh-ni hsien-ning shih-mo chi (A Complete Account of the Fall of Hai-
ning to the Kwangtung Rebels in 1860 and 1861) by Ch'en Hsi-chi, a
chin-shih of the same district, who recorded in considerable detail the
heavy suffering the war imposed upon the people and the Taipings' brave
action in both attacking and defending the city of Hai-ning; the Kuei-
ch'ou Chung-chou li-ping chi-lüeh (A Brief Account of Military Disaster
in Honan, 1853) by Ch'en Shan-chün, who was then a spectator of the development of the Taipings' northern expedition in Honan; the Keng-shen
pi-luan shih-lu (A True Account of Suppressing the Rebellion in 1860)
by Chao Wei-fu, who described the military and social conditions of the
province of Chekiang, especially at the cities of Suchow and Hangchow,
and gave a frank criticism of the corruption and inefficiency of the
government forces; the Yüeh-chou chi-lüeh (Brief Notes about Shaohsing)
which the Taipings attacked in October 1861 and kept under their

jurisdiction until the early part of the next year, by an anonymous
writer who gives a little sketch of the Taiping military, social, and
political organizations and the troubles of the government troops who
were more cruel and harmful than their enemies; the Chien-tê-chai sui-pi
(Desultory Notes of Chien-tê-chai) by Hu Chang-lin who kept a record of
the events during the Taipings' occupation of Chang-hsing, Chekiang,
from March 1860 to October 1862 when the Taipings' new calendar was enforced in that area and cannibalism was said to have been practiced.
The last document is Kan-wang Hung Jen-kan teng k'ou-kung (Affidavits
of Prince Kan, Hung Jen-Kan, and Others) based on the original block-
print version. The third part of Hsieh's work is a collection of
poems and ballads depicting the sad stories of Taiping military developments, but these vague poetic descriptions are hard to use for
historical narration.

One of Hsieh's strong points is his wide knowledge of individual
and unauthorized writings. He has a beautiful style in handling miscellaneous materials and reproducing a fluent story. However, he
seems to lack scientific and foreign language training. He has made
more mistakes than other experts. Consequently his contribution to
Taiping history is in his long years of painstaking research. There
is an abundance of information in his productivity, but a dearth of
originality and accuracy.

3. Lo Erh-kang

Lo Erh-kang is another authority of the Taiping period. He was
born in Kuei-hsien, Kwangsi, and began the study of this history in
1932, keeping up his interest with little digression. He has been
a member of the Institute of Social Sciences, Academia Sinica, for
many years and that position has probably given him the opportunity
to devote his time to research. His avowed purpose is to make a
thorough and critical examination of all facets and problems of
Taiping history, and thereafter he plans to compile a monumental
work on it. He has published more than other specialists on the subject. His T'ai-p'ing T'ien-kuo shih-kang (Outline History of the
Heavenly Kingdom of Great Peace, the Commercial Press, 1937), paying

attention to the cause and effect of the movement, has been generally considered one of the best elementary textbooks. The T'ai-p'ing T'ien-kuo shih ts'ung-k'ao (Miscellaneous Studies of the Taiping history, first published in 1944, second printing 1947 by the Cheng-chung shu-chü) is a work in which eighteen articles written before 1936 are collected. The author is very proud of his "Hung Ta-ch'üan k'ao" (A Study of Hung Ta-ch'üan), but his conclusion may require further consideration. His investigation of the problem of Chu Chiu-tao is important because it touches on the connection between the secret societies and the God-worshippers. The last article also has value for it introduces some new materials about the Taiping from the un-published memorials of Hsiang Jung (d. 1856) who was a high Manchu commander attempting to suppress the rebellion.

Lo has written a short biography of Hung Hsiu-ch'üan, Hung Hsiu-ch'üan chüan with appendixes on Shih Ta-k'ai and Li Hsiu-ch'eng.[4] He intended to write a popular book giving very bright pictures of the revolutionary leaders. Perhaps they are painted a little too bright. There is a mistake on page 54, stating that the Taipings' entrance to Shansi was to find a high topography in order to attack Peking. As a matter of fact they were compelled to make the detour. The Chin-t'ien ch'i-i-ch'ien Hung Hsiu-ch'üan nien-p'u (A Chronological Biography of Hung Hsiu-ch'üan before he started the revolution at Chin-t'ien)[5] is a year-by-year history of the early life and the political and social background of Hung compiled by Lo and his wife. It is very poorly printed and its contribution is limited.

Apart from these works, Lo Erh-kang's T'ien-ti-hui wen-hsien-lu (Documents and Notes of the Society of Heaven and Earth, published by the Cheng-chung shu-chü, 1943) contains significant and inside stories about the secret society, and the compiler's notes, stressing the in-fluence of the Shui-hu-ch'üan or "All Men are Brothers" on the forma-tion of Chinese secret societies, are interesting. His Hsiang-chün hsin-chih (A New Account of the Hunan Braves, the Commercial Press, 1939) and his detailed survey of the Lu-ying ping-chih (An Account of the Army of the Green Standard, the Commercial Press, 1944) have direct bearing on Taiping history. The latter work is in a new field not

extensively explored by earlier scholars. Unfortunately Tseng's
water force does not receive due attention in the first treatise.

Through the courtesy of Mr. Lo, three of his recent publications
were received in May 1949. The most important of the three is the
T'ai-p'ing T'ien-kuo shih k'ao-cheng chi (A Collection of Critical
Essays on the Taiping history published by Cheng-chung shu-chü in
October, 1948). It is divided into five parts: the first is a
critical study of the historical events such as the history of the
beginning of the revolution at Chin-t'ien, the women's camp, the internal struggle between the East and North kings, and so on; the
second part is a discussion of the Taiping calendar consisting of the
author's correspondence with Tung Tso-pin dealing with the making
of the new calendar; the third and fourth parts are a collection of
essays on authenticity, editions, or notes on various kinds of the
writings or inscriptions written by or dealing with the Taiping
leaders; and the last part contains notes of the author's field
investigations of Chin-t'ien and other spots. More evidence is
given on Hung Ta-ch'üan[6] to support the author's thesis of the nonexistence of the person and the lack of relation between the early
Taiping leaders and the members of secret societies. Whether this
thesis is sound or not will be discussed in the following pages.
The most significant entry should be the comparison of Li Hsiu-ch'eng's
"autobiography," common edition, with the original manuscript kept
in the hands of Tseng Kuo-fan's descendants in Hunan. Unfortunately
the statements about the rare manuscript are too general and vague
to satisfy the eager desire of a bibliophile or historian. It is
hoped that the original manuscript will be reproduced by photolithography or a more detailed comparison made. The other two publications, one on the Taiping metal and stone inscriptions, and the
other on the early history at Kwangsi are less important.[7]

Lo Erh-kang has had a few other works in manuscript form in the
hands of the publisher for a long time. He has been kind enough to
give the writer a detailed table of contents of each of his unpublished
works.[8]

Before the publication of all Lo's works, it is, however, not

safe to judge or make a definite evaluation of his contribution.
His strong point is his critical spirit demonstrated in sifting the
reliable from the unreliable, a spirit Lo gratefully acknowledged to
have been received from his teacher Hu Shih.[9] Dr. Hu, however,
criticised Lo for giving all credit to the Taipings, and neglecting
their wanton destruction.[10] Suffice it here to say that from what Lo
has published and what he has planned to do, he may be considered the
greatest Chinese Taiping historian, even though some of his conclusions
reached from critical study still have to be reconsidered or accepted
with caution. His publications are rather miscellaneous with over-
lapping or duplicating due obviously to the pressure of poverty.
Lo Erh-kang is certainly the most productive authority on Taiping
history.

4. Kuo T'ing-i

Another assiduous worker on Taiping history is Kuo T'ing-i who has
also spent more than ten years on this period and whose publications
are the T'ai-p'ing T'ien-kuo li-fa k'ao-cheng (A Critical Examination
of the Calendar System of the Taiping T'ien-kuo, the Commercial Press,
1937) and the T'ai-p'ing T'ien-kuo shih-shih jih-chih (A Day by Day
Record of the History of the Heavenly Kingdom of Great Peace published
in 1946 by the Commercial Press, two volumes).[11] The former work makes
a distinguished contribution to the concurrence of the Taiping calendar,
and the latter shows much painstaking research including an annotated
bibliography and much correlated information. Consequently the two are
indispensable reference works for any student of Taiping history even
though the style is occasionally not very readable and his point of
view toward problematic events is usually half way between Hsieh and Lo.

5. P'eng Tse-i

P'eng Tse-i is another promising student of the Taiping history
whose T'ai-p'ing T'ien-kuo kê-ming ssu-ch'ao (The Revolutionary Thought
of the Taipings, the Commercial Press, 1946) deserves our attention.
P'eng is also a member of the Institute of Social Sciences, Academia
Sinica. His approach to the history is different from others in that
he stresses the ideological side of the Taipings. Although he has

published only the book just mentioned, he has distinguished himself as a careful writer. He is the scholar who suspected that the year 1836 was not the correct date for Hung Hsiu-ch'üan to receive the nine religious books, because in that year P'eng found that Liang A-fa was not in Canton. G. F. Hudson's idea, "the civil war had indeed the character of a war of religion" is condemned as wrong (p. 23) by P'eng who can use both Chinese and English sources. However, owing to limited access to Western books, the author is obliged to rely a great deal on bibliographical data from Kenneth S. Latourette's History of Christian Missions in China. He will make greater contributions when he has more Western sources available. Many sections in this book have been published as magazine articles.

6. Hsiao I-shan

We must now note the senior scholar of Ch'ing history, Hsiao I-shan whose contribution to the study of the Taiping rebellion lies in his publication of the T'ai-p'ing T'ien-kuo ts'ung-shu which has been mentioned above. With this fine publication, which has a brief preface or postface for each document, most of the Taiping official works are made available to the public. Hsiao is a voluminous writer of Ch'ing history and he has published many short essays dealing with the Taiping in the periodical, Ching-shih and in the collection of his essays entitled Fei-yü-kuan wen-ts'un.[12] While other Chinese Taiping historians are largely poverty-stricken, Hsiao was well financed by Chiang Kai-shek to travel to Europe and America and was thus given a chance to collect material abroad. Unfortunately, his strong political interest reduces the quality of his academic work even though he has collected a great deal of material. Some of his bibliographical notes or postfaces to Taiping documents seem to be written extempore with little insight into the text.

7. Other Historians' Work on the Period

Finally a communist publication on the Taiping movement merits our attention. The book is called T'ai-p'ing T'ien-kuo kê-ming yün-tung by Fan Wen-lan, who had been professor of Chinese and history at several universities in Peiping and Tientsin before he went to the communist area, and author of a few works on Chinese history.[13] His treatise on the Taiping is simple and clear and he has made astute interpretations of the causes of and the motives for Hung Hsiu-ch'üan's writings. As a long-time, practical revolutionist, he understands the inside story and the surrounding environment much better and clearer than other armchair writers. Although Fan is a communist, this work, like his general history of China, is not very radical, but is quite objective and scientific even though the author has perhaps unconsciously a viewpoint of learning a lesson from the Taiping revolution as a reference for the present movement. With little access to primary sources, he is obliged to use many secondary sources and is not entirely free from errors. In spite of these, Fan Wen-lan's T'ai-p'ing T'ien-kuo kê-ming yün-tung and Lo Erh-kang's T'ai-p'ing T'ien-kuo shih-kang are probably the two best general treatments of the famous subject.

Besides the authors mentioned above, the prolific writer Chu Ch'ien-chih, professor and chairman of the National Sun Yat-sen University, Canton, Liang Hu-lu, and a number of others have written articles or books discussing Taiping history. We regret that there is no space to mention them one by one.

8. Japanese Works

Japanese scholars have not been so enthusiastic in analyzing the Taiping revolution as they have been about other facets of modern China. Although Naito and Inaba (q.v.) pioneered the road to Taiping sources, the progress made in the pursuit of their history seems to be not very great. There are, however, many books and articles directly or indirectly about the Taipings either written in Japanese or translated from Chinese and English. There are also a number of contemporary accounts, some of which are written in formal style and some informal and unorthodox.[14] A twenty-page bibliography of all types of material about the Taiping has been prepared.[15]

Among the noteworthy authors, it is necessary to mention

Nashimoto Yūhei, _Taihei Tengoku kakumei_ (1942), Sano Gaku, _Taihei Tengoku kakumei_ (1947), and Toyama Gunji, _Taihei Tengoku no Shanghai_ (1947). The first book was written during the author's stay at Peking. It is a general and proportional narration of the whole period, with considerable emphasis on the political, economic and social systems. There is no mention of Taiping effect and influence. The chart of the main facts of the T'ai-p'ing T'ien-kuo is too brief to have much use. Nor is there any footnote or any unusual work quoted in the narration. The author, however, who seems to have read most of the common works on this period, made use of recent research by Japanese scholars and explained everything clearly in 440 pages for the layman as well as the expert. Sano was formerly a communist and was put in jail for some time. In this book the Taiping history is rather superficially interpreted from the leftist point of view. Its chief merit lies in his use of individual correspondence, memorials, and current essays which are not often used. As for Toyama's work, it is a general survey of the Taiping's relation with Shanghai and their diplomatic relations with foreign powers. Some materials are drawn from the _Ch'ing-tai ch'ou-pan i-wu shih-mo_, and a few Japanese works of fictions; H. B. Morse's _In the Days of the Taipings_ is also frequently quoted. There is no particular material, interpretation, or point of view in Komparu's book.

Many good discussions on the Taiping are chapters in large volumes. The chapter on the Taiping in Inaba Iwakichi's _Ch'ing-ch'ao ch'üan-shih_ (translated into Chinese by Tan Tao) is one of the earliest treatises of the subject and is still useful, though not without errors. Yano Nūchi, _Kindai Shina-shi_ (1926) has three chapters (pp. 284-413) giving a detailed description of the Taiping military development. He used the _Kuang-chou fu-chih_ to trace the activity of the San-ho-hui or the triad in the Hsiang-shan district. Nohara Shirō in _Sekai rekishi taikei_, volume 9 (1934), and the article on Taiping T'ien-kuo by Masui [Tsuneo] contributed to the _Tōyō rekishi daijiten_ (1938, vol. 5, pp. 503-508) are both terse summaries for encyclopedic use. Masui Tsuneo is still devoting his time and energy to the pursuit of Taiping history. Toriyama Kiichi in _Tōhō bunkashi sōkō_ (1935) recognizes that the Taiping movement has the same nature as the White Lotus society and other religious forces in Chinese history. Sano Kesami, Shina kin hyakunen shi (1939) has devoted the fourth chapter of volume one (pp. 255-309) to the Taiping movement and pays close attention to the economic background, but except for this point, there is nothing of particular value either in source material or in interpretation.

There are also a number of good magazine articles written by famous scholars. In order to keep this essay fairly readable, they are given in the footnote.[16]

9. English Sources

In English there are twenty-odd contemporary accounts of the Taiping rebellion. Among them the best ones seem to be: The Visions of Hung-Siu-tshuen and Origin of the Kwangsi Insurrection (Hongkong, 1854) by Theodore Hamberg, although I do not think that everything said in this book is true, because it is somewhat like an official biography which usually tends to gloss over mistakes or undesirable events; The History of the Insurrection in China, with Notices of Christianity, Creed, and Proclamations of the Insurgents by M. M. Callery and Yvan, translated in English with a supplementary chapter by John Oxenford, (London, 1854) is informative though full of errors; The Chinese and Their Rebellions by Thomas T. Meadows (London, 1856) is sympathetic to the Taipings; The Taiping Rebellion in China by Lindesay Brine (London, 1862) is probably the best of all, because of its fair attitude and adequate description, and seems to be worth translating into Chinese. The Ti-ping Tien-kwok, the History of the Ti-ping Revolution including a narrative of the author's personal adventures by Lin-Le [Augustus F. Lindley] has been translated into Chinese by Meng Hsien-cheng, entitled T'ai-p'ing T'ien-kuo wai-chi. This is not so good as Brine's work and has been criticised as "a rather untrustworthy record,"[17] but written from the viewpoint of a spokesman for the Taiping, the author's numerous quotations plus his first hand information make this work worth consulting. The Life of T'ai-p'ing-wang, Chief of the Chinese Insurrection by John Milton Mackie (New York, 1857) is also a fairly good book. Although there are some errors, it has an appendix containing many original documents translated into English.

The accounts of the Taipings by contemporary observers gradually gave way to accounts of the "Ever-Victorious Army," and especially of the exploits of Chinese Gordon, concerning whom and other members of the family so many biographies have been produced, that there is a Bibliography of the Gordons.[18]

The period of Gordon-admiration created such an impression among Westerners that they thought it was the Ever-Victorious Army alone which suppressed the Taiping Rebellion. The credit for correcting such an inaccurate idea should be given to William James Hail whose Tseng Kuo-fan and the Taiping Rebellion (New Haven, 1927) uses Chinese sources and makes Tseng's career very prominent. Sometimes the author's English leaves room for improvement. In spite of the fact that Hail's thesis or factual presentation has been generally accepted for more than two decades, a textbook on Eastern Asia still holds to the old idea that the Ever-Victorious Army was almost the only force which wiped out the Taipings.[19]

Another distinguished contribution to the Taiping movement is made by G. E. Taylor whose article, "The Taiping Rebellion, its Economic Background and Social Theory" in The Chinese Social and Political Science Review, XVI[20] is one of the earliest attempts to make a scientific in- terpretation of the rebellion with emphasis on its economic and social background. Even today when so many more documents have been made avail- able and more works have been produced, this article, which has been translated into Japanese, is still useful. Now under the direction of G. E. Taylor, the Far Eastern Institute of the University of Washing- ton, Seattle, is doing a systematic study of the Taiping Revolution and modern Chinese history in cooperation with several Chinese scholars. It is hoped that the world will soon profit by their publications.

10. French and German Sources

In French, although M. M. Callery and Yvan wrote L'Insurrection en Chine depuis son origine jusqu'a la prise de Nankin, and a number of Taiping documents are preserved in the Bibliothèque Nationale, there are not many studies on the Taipings except for a few on their approach to Shanghai which was of direct concern to the French. Apart from Henri Cordier's Histoire des relations de la Chine avec les puissances occidentales, 1860-1896 (1901-1902) in which there are four chapters in volume one giving a succinct narration of the Taiping developments with some quotations from original sources including the letters of the Reverend I. J. Roberts, there are other works such as Charles B. Maybon's Histoire de la concession Français de Changhai, (Paris, 1929) which is an important work on Taiping diplomacy. This book makes extensive use of the North China Herald and other contemporary papers. Arthur Millac's (pseud.) Les Francais à Changhai en 1853-1855, Episodes du siège de Changhai par les impériaux, (Paris, 1884), is a short narrative of the Triad occupation of the city.[21]

Not many German books on the Taiping are either listed in H. Cordier's Bibliotheca Sinica or collected in the Library of Congress or the Harvard University Library. There are, however, two works of considerable importance. One is C. Spielmann, Die Taiping-revolution in China (1850-1864).[22] The author is anti-British, as Germany at that time did not have any interest of her own in China. Spielmann's judgment is quite objective, although his presentation in many respects is polemic. He condemns the British and French intervention as well as the Manchu corruption, and praises the Taiping policy toward women, education, opium prohibition, and slavery. He perceives the Taiping religion as early Christianity on a communist basis. He maintains that the real reason for British interference was the opium trade (p. 78 and passim); the strategy of Prince Kung was to grant permission for the opium trade in order to get the support of the British and French and maneuver them into a position to strengthen the Manchus (pp. 95, 135). He thinks that the Boxer rebellion and anti-foreign attitude of the Chinese would not have occurred if the Taipings had won (III). In short the book has some good ideas and is also an important source on Taiping diplomatic affairs.

Another German book is Wilhelm Oehler: Die Taiping-Bewegung: Geschichte eines chinesisch-christlichen Gottesreichs (Gütersloh, 1923). The author says that he used only important German sources including Basler Magazin für die neuste Geschichte der evangelische,

Missions und Bibelgesellschaft (1854), and Basler Evangelisches Missions magazin, Neue Folge, Herausgegeben von Dr. Ostertag 1861-64. He also consulted the works of Spielmann, Ku Hung-ming, Li Hung-chang, Neumark, and Hamberg. Unfortunately Oehler looks at the problem from a missionary point of view and comes to the conclusion that had China been converted to Christianity it would have been better off. Foreign opposition to the Taipings is revealed by a letter of Bruce to Russell on June 23, 1860, saying that the British would lose pawned customs receipts if the Taipings got control of port cities (p. 154). Apparently concubinage of the various wangs changed the previous favorable impressions of some missionary circles to anti-Taiping sentiment in 1863 (pp. 156-57, 224-25). Apart from these points the book contributes little.[23]

11. Russian Source

Russian material about the Taipings is also scarce,[24] even though Marx and Engels mentioned the awakening of China, and since the 1920's the Soviet historians are reported to have paid considerable attention to the peasant war. In the Library of Congress the only entry on this subject is a small book published in Moscow in 1941 under the title: Taipiny; velikoe Krestianskoe i Taipinskoe gosudarstvo v Kitae, 1850-1864 (The Taipings; the Great Peasant War and the Taiping State in China) written by G. S. Kara-Murza. The table of contents may be translated as follows:

    Feudal China Before the Great Peasant War
    The Beginning of the Rising
    The Campaigns of the Taiping Army
    The Rebellions of the "Triads" and "Torch-bearers."
      The Collapse of the Manchu Empire
    The Taiping State (1853-1854)
    The First Defeats of the Taipings. The Taiping
      State in the Years 1854-1860
    The Anglo-French Intervention, 1862-1864
    The Historical Significance of the Great Peasant War

The value of this book does not lie in any footnote or bibliography, but in its new ideas. It is written for the public, not for scholars. According to the author, in the middle of the 19th century, Europe was capitalistic, while China was still in the stage of feudalism

(p. 3). The historical and social background is succinctly presented in pages 3 to 20, and the rapid rise in the silver price is stressed. In 1830 one tael of silver was worth 1000 coins; in 1848 it jumped to 2000, and in 1851, to 4700. The inflation caused rises in prices and in land rent. The Christian doctrine preached by Hung remained an ideological veneer under which was hidden the protest of the Chinese peasants against feudalism (p. 28). The members of the Triad Society composed of peasants, artisans, and merchants were dissatisfied with the feudalistic exploitation. The merchant class and the gentry joined the movement, because they did not form part of the feudalistic hierarchy, and owing to the lack of a working proletariat it was possible for them to do so. Unfortunately the Taiping leaders themselves became feudalists. At the time of the rebellion there existed no working class in the modern sense of the word, who could have taken over the leadership in the rebellion (p. 121). Although the Taipings controlled a large part of China, the Taiping peasant communism was utopian. Kara-Murza says that this utopian idea was influenced by the works of Thomas More, Saint Simon, F. Campanelli, and Francois Fourier (p. 122). This statement, however, is dubious.

The Anglo-French intervention worked out by the Manchus seems to be considered by Kara-Murza very detrimental to the Taiping movement. In 1853 the Russian writer Goncharov visited Shanghai and reported on the ruthless British attitude of treating the Chinese like "human cattle." In the same year the Russian scholar Skachkov lived in Peking where he asked a Chinese whether or not he thought the Taipings would come to the capital, and the reply was that they would come and he was not afraid of their advent. The Mandarins tried to scare British and other merchants about their trade, because of the Taiping menace (pp. 67-68). The Taiping attack on Shanghai in August 1860 was opposed by Manchu followers as well as by Anglo-French troops. The foreign interventionists not only took military action, but also tried to deprive the Taipings of food provisions in cities, which is regarded by the author as "barbarous action." Tsarist Russia gave the Manchus fifty cannons and considerable funds to combat the revolutionists (p. 110). The Manchus linked up with the foreign colonial powers in order to overcome the Taipings and China

quickly became a victim of the European capitalistic nations, a
semi-colony.

This is the gist of the little Russian book on the Taiping. The
work is a systematic, factual summary interwoven with the theories of
Soviet Russia. Some day the book may be translated into English or
Chinese to show some difference from ordinary narration.

III. NEW LIGHT ON A FEW KNOTTY PROBLEMS

1. The Problem of Hung Ta-ch'üan

One of the oldest and most difficult problems of Taiping history
is whether or not there was a leader by the name of Hung Ta-ch'üan who
was entitled T'ien-tê-wang or King of Heavenly Virtue, and whether his
confessions are authentic or not. The problem has existed since 1852
when Western sources either had Hung Hsiu-ch'üan and T'ien-tê-wang mixed
as one person[1] or doubted the existence of the person and the authenticity of the confessions.[2] The question has remained in argument
ever since.

Chinese sources indicate that when Hung Ta-ch'üan was escorted
from Kwangsi to Peking, a censor had declared that he was not an
important leader and that his significance was exaggerated so as to
compensate for the repeated failure of the government forces in Kwangsi.
Consequently, Emperor Wen-tsung proclaimed a decree on May 17, 1852,
in which Hung Ta-ch'üan was acknowledged as an adherent, not as a
leader of the rebels.[3] In 1905 an effective statement denounced this
fiction[4] and in 1922 Liang Ch'i-ch'ao in his Research Method of Chinese
History said emphatically that sometimes a story was completely fabricated but gradually became a primary source with no way to disprove it
such as the history of the rebel leader, Hung Ta-ch'üan.[5] Now let us
briefly examine the arguments on both sides of the long pending case.

A. Arguments to Prove the Nonexistence of Hung Ta-ch'üan and the
Fabrication of his Confessions.

In 1934 while reviewing the Tsei-ch'ing hui-tsuan, Lo Erh-kang
charged that there was no T'ien-tê-wang, Hung Ta-ch'üan, because (1)
the name was not mentioned when several kings were created at Yung-an,
(2) the title, T'ien-tê-wang, was contradictory to the tenets of Taiping
religion, (3) the facts about Hung Ta-ch'üan were completely neglected
in Li Hsiu-ch'eng's confession, (4) officials and scholars at that
time did not recognize Hung as an important Taiping leader, (5) a
memorial was submitted to the emperor by a courtier alleging that the

report of the capture had been exaggerated for the purpose of obtain-
ing a reward, (6) the emperor issued a decree acknowledging Hung Ta-ch'üan
as an adherent and not a leader of the rebels, and (7) the confessions
did not agree with the historical development of the Taipings.[6]

B. Arguments to Prove the Existence of Hung Ta-ch'üan.

The reasons for believing in the actuality of Hung Ta-ch'üan were
remarkably presented by Yü Ta-kang, a history student of Kuang-hua
University and of Yenching Graduate School. Yü's mother, a descendant
of Tseng Kuo-fan, was thoroughly versed in Taiping stories, and his
brother, Yü Ta-wei, collected much Taiping material from Germany. In
response to Lo's accusations, Yü pointed out that Hung Ta-ch'üan's confessions generally agree with the early history of the Taipings, which
information was not then available to government circles. At that time
the Taipings were harassed; the Manchu generals on the front faithfully
reported their successes and failures, and there was no necessity to
create a fabricated victory for getting a reward. Lo's fourth, fifth,
and sixth points fundamentally cannot prove the nonexistence of Hung
Ta-ch'üan among the Taipings. The first and seventh accusations do
not affect Hung Ta-ch'üan whose position was equal to that of Hung Hsiu-
ch'üan, but superior to other princes. As to the second and third points,
Hung was respected as a T'ien-te, an original title of the secret society,
San-ho-hui or Triad, and his rank was not bestowed by the Taipings. The
selection of members was not strict until the Taiping flight from Yung-an
when members with different political and religious background were
gradually sifted out. That was the natural result of the struggle between a national movement to restore the Ming and a religious-fanatic
reform movement. After the party cleaning, Hung Ta-ch'üan's name was
seldom mentioned by Taiping leaders, who did not admit that they had
once cooperated with members of secret societies.

In addition Yü pointed out that the picture of T'ien-tê wearing
Ming costume in the front of the book by Callery and Yvan who got it
from Kwangsi, is reproduced by Inaha Iwakichi as the image of Hung
Hsiu-ch'üan, whose official costume did not imitate the Ming but who
usually wore a wind-cap, as mentioned in Hung Ta-ch'üan's confession.

This is proof that there was such a person as Hung Ta-ch'üan,[7] and is a keen observation.

C. Lo's Rebuttal

After the first round of argument in 1934 Lo delivered a long rebuttal, upon completing two years of painstaking research, under the title, "A Study of Hung Ta-ch'üan."[8] In this article he brings forth the discrepancy between Hung's confession made before General Sai-shang-a (d. 1875), an Imperial Commissioner to Kwangsi and Commander-in-chief of the suppression of the rebellion, and another confession made before a joint examination committee of Grand Councillors and the Ministry of Punishment. The former, about 1600 words long, was a written confession; the latter, about 490 words long, was written by the examiners. A comparison of the two documents shows the discrepancies of personal name, native place, date of joining the Taipings and official titles. Lo thinks that the Peking confession was purposely modified by the ministers to help Sai-shang-a. In the Kwangsi confession, Lo finds errors about (1) the founding of the Association of God-worshipping, (2) the native place of Wei Ch'ang-hui, Hsiao Ch'ao-kuei, and Yang Hsiu-ch'ing, (3) the bestowal of ranks on Shih Ta-k'ai, Ch'in Jih-ch'ang, and others, (4) the title of T'ien-tê-wang, which is contradictory to the Taiping theocracy, (5) the address of "elder brother" which was only applied to Jesus Christ — no one less had the privilege of being so addressed, (6) and (7) and finally, Hung's report of the Taiping calendar and the date of the order to raise the siege is not exact. Lo believes that the Kwangsi confession was forged by Sai-shang-a with extreme care and over-all consideration. Unfortunately, there are still leaks to be discovered. Sai-shang-a forged the document to gloss over his failure. He secured the intimate information about the rebels from captured materials such as calendars, religious works, costumes, intelligence, and confessions of other captives. Lo believes that Hung Ta-ch'üan was merely an educated man captured by and retained to do some clerical work for the Taipings.

The name and its importance were all fabricated by Sai-shang-a to suit his purposes. This is the gist of Lo Erh-kang's contention.

In another work, T'ai-p'ing Tien-kuo shih k'ao-cheng chi, Lo supplies additional material in support of his thesis. One of the officers, who escorted Hung Ta-ch'üan to Peking, gave some secret medicine to the captive so that he could not talk when he reached Peking and thus all confessions were fabricated. Lo considers this story "very reasonable" and a strong side-proof of his interpretation.

Lo's arguments are well documented and are sufficient to answer Yü's points indirectly. His assiduous work should be recognized with applause. Nevertheless, after reading over the long article, one may not be deeply impressed and thoroughly convinced, because some of the errors cavilled at are very minute and there are contradictory arguments, an example of which is that in the first part the author tries to prove the nonexistence of the person and the event and the error of official titles, and in the latter part he describes the person, his dress, and information concerning similar official titles. Sai-shang-a's knowledge of the insurgents expressed in his memorials to the emperor before and after Hung's arrest was much more meager and hesitant than the content of the confession. Now let us see the opinions of other scholars.

D. Opinions of Other Taiping Historians

Opinions on the enigma of Hung Ta-ch'üan are divergent. Hsieh Hsing-yao,[9] and Hsiao I-shan[10] maintain the existence of Hung and the authenticity of the confession. Lo Erh-kang and Chu Chien-chih[11] deny the existence of the man and the event. Three other scholars have made a compromise. William James Hail believes that the confession is genuine, although "one must not ignore the fact that there are a number of inaccuracies and glaring mistakes," and Hung Ta-ch'üan's real name was Chu Chiu-t'ao, a leader of a secret society.[12] Kuo T'ing-i believed in 1937 that there was actually a Hung Ta-ch'üan, a member of the Heaven and Earth Society, but not necessarily an important figure. At the beginning of the revolution, secret societies were very active in Kwangtung and Kwangsi. The Taipings made use of the reign-title,

T'ien-tê, which was given to the opportunist Hung Ta-ch'üan who did not thoroughly understand either the important policies of the Taipings or the secret dealings of the Triad and therefore some errors are apparent in the confession.[13] In 1944 Kuo added[14] that Hung Ta-ch'üan's real name was Chiao Liang,[15] an ambitious, fanatic Hunanese and a member of the Heaven and Earth Society.

The best attempt to ascertain the truth has been made by Chien Yu-wen who maintains that the confessions are largely genuine with quite a number of changes interjected by Sai-shang-a and the Peking examiners; that Hung Ta-ch'üan was Chiao Liang or Chiao Ta, a native of Hsing-ning, Hunan; that Chu Chiu-t'ao was Ch'iu Ch'ang-tao, also a leader of secret societies, and that the famous poem in the confession is also proved authentic.[16] Chien's terse and candid presentation of evidence and arguments is quite convincing.

E. A Brief Personal Remark

After reading the written confession many times, we can hardly believe that it is entirely apocryphal, whereas the Peking confession seems to have been scamped by some clerk during or after the examination. There was no strong motive for Sai-shang-a to fabricate the person and the event, since, according to the Ch'ing-shih-lu, before the Yungan battles several victories were reported to the emperor who was quite pleased with developments and after Hung's capture only a second captain was rewarded, Sai even being degraded four ranks because of the flight of the insurgents and the attack on Kuei-lin.[17] There-fore in the light of the present research and available documents,[18] Chien's conclusion is acceptable.

2. The Problem of Taiping Connections with Secret Societies

In close connection with the Hung Ta-ch'üan problem is the Taiping relation with the T'ien-ti-hui, or San-ho-hui, or San-tien-hui. Many Taiping experts like Hsieh, Hsiao, Yü, and Hail feel that at the be-ginning of the revolution the rebel leaders had for a time some alliance with the Heaven and Earth society, but after the capture of Hung Ta-ch'üan

the bond was denied and the name was banned in Taiping literature,
and that thereafter the Taipings barred the members of secret
societies. Mao I-heng regarded the God-worshippers as a branch of
the Heaven and Earth society, and Hung Hsiu-ch'üan was first entitled
T'ai-p'ing wang, later changed to Heavenly King. Hung's religious
ideas are full of superstitions and practices from secret societies.[19]
Kuo T'ing-i is of the opinion that at the inception of Hung Hsiu-ch'üan's
movement he was not without relations with the Triad members, many of
whom joined the Taipings.[20] Wang Chung-min remains neutral; that is,
he neither proves nor disproves the connection between the two factions,
while Lo Erh-kang and Chien Yu-wen stoutly support the interpretation
that the Taipings and secret societies were utterly independent groups.

A. Opinions Disproving the Connection

The most convincing evidence against the connection is found in
Hung Hsiu-ch'üan's own words given in Theodore Hamberg's book:

> "Though I never entered the Triad Society, I have often
> heard it said that their object is to subvert the Tsing and
> restore the Ming dynasty. Such an expression was very
> proper in the time of Khang-hi, when this society was at
> first formed, but now after the lapse of two hundred years,
> we may still speak of subverting the Tsing, but we cannot
> properly speak of restoring the Ming. At all events, when
> our native mountains and rivers are recovered, a new dynasty
> must be established.... There are several evil practices
> connected with the Triad Society, which I detest; if any
> new member enter the society, he must worship the devil, and
> utter thirty-six oaths; a sword is placed upon his neck, and
> he is forced to contribute money for the use of the society..."[21]

This statement is sufficient to obliterate many stories about the
Heavenly King's dealings with society members who, from beginning to end,
were admitted to his camp only on grounds of abandoning their original
practices and obeying the religious and political doctrines of the new
master. The members of the Triad in Kwangsi lacked a unified leadership, whereas the God-worshippers' force was the most formidable enemy
of the imperial party. This is Lo Erh-kang's main idea on the subject.[22]
Chien Yu-wen augments Lo's views by saying that Chinese and Western
sources are often under the misapprehension that (1) the Taipings were

a metamorphosis of the Triad society, (2) that they had special relations with the prevalent secret societies and that they made alliances
with the Triad society, both when Hung Hsiu-ch'üan and Hung Ta-ch'üan
were first co-sovereigns, and after they separated. Such queer and
unsupported statements are caused by ignorance of the early history
of the two parties and by the fact that in the early years of the
turmoil the secret members in scattered areas mistook the victory of
others as their own, and so responded and made public proclamations
by using the popular reign-title, T'ien-tê. Chien sums up his investigations in one sentence, that is, from beginning to end, the God-
worshippers were God-worshippers, while the secret society members were
also independent. The two should not be confused. There was neither
alliance nor cooperative relationship between them, nor were the two
Hungs co-sovereigns who ruled shoulder to shoulder in their separate
spheres of influence. From a religious point of view, the Taipings
stubbornly stuck to one God; the secret societies worshipped many gods.
On the ethical side the Taipings had strict discipline; opium, tobacco,
gambling, adultery, plundering, slaughter and disturbance of people
were at first strictly forbidden, whereas the secret society members
had no such inhibitions and were very unprincipled. In political aims,
the Taipings desired to establish a new dynasty of theocracy; the
secret society members insisted on restoring the Ming to the Chu family.

Apart from these three fundamental differences to keep the two
factions divided, their organization, their actual strength, and
their supernatural power made the Taipings look down on the other
groups, and ashamed to cooperate with them.[23]

B. Influence of the Secret Societies on the Taipings.

In the light of so many new materials about early Taiping history
discovered in the last decade, the problem is not as dark as before.
As a matter of fact the confusion was well-nigh cleared up by Brine
long ago, who wrote:

> "In the several articles devoted to the subject of the then
> little known and less understood rebellion, which appeared
> in the English papers published in China between 1849 and

1853 a great deal of space is given up to ingenious
articles by writers who wished to show that the rebellion was an offshoot of the well-known Triad Society.
It has since been proved that the Taipings have nothing
to say to the Triads, who, however, at one time, early
in the movement, temporarily joined it...."[24]

Our opinion is, in brief, that after turning over the pages of
the Ch'ing-shih-lu for this period, one must be deeply impressed by
the fact that the activities of the secret societies of various
denominations and the so-called "bandits" in Kwangsi, Kwangtung,
Hunan, and other areas had actually paved the way for the Taiping
movement. Although no permanent, formal alliance was made, the
Taipings must have had at least some informal association and
received some indirect influence and stimulation from the secret
societies, such as the adoption of confidential signs and language
parallel to those used by them,[25] and the acceptance of a large number
of society members,[26] whose activities formed one of the most important causes of the Rebellion. Their poorly organized riots preceded,
paralleled and outlived the Taipings,[27] who failed to offer close
cooperation or help when the Triads occupied Shanghai, Amoy, and
some cities near Canton, and that desiccated the whole Taiping strength.
In Chinese history it is not uncommon for a successful rebel leader
to minimize or deny the contributions of contemporary, coordinate, or
cooperative forces, as Han Kao-tsu did to Hsiang Yü, Ming Tai-tsu to
other "bandit chiefs," and the Kuomintang to the influence of the May 4th
Movement of 1919. It is therefore easy to understand that the Taiping
relation with secret societies had already been reduced to a minimum.
Modern writers sympathetic to the Taiping tend to go even further.
But in the T'ien-ch'ing tao-li-shu, which is a very important official
publication of their early history, there are many instances of dealings with the members of the secret societies, and Lo Tai-kang with
his force obviously cooperated with Hung from beginning to end.

On the other hand, their religion was described as spoiled by
secret society members joining the Taipings. As Arthur Moule says:

"This force was subsequently swollen by very many recruits
from the White Lotus, and other secret political societies;

and it is worth observing that the accession of these motley crowds, most of whom were without any religion at all, or devoted adherents of the God of War, must have exerted a powerful influence in neutralising and eventually obliterating the spiritual elements in the earliest bands which I noticed above."[28]

Thus in spite of the lack of clear mention of direct connections and close alliance, a conservative conclusion is that the Taipings received both good and bad influence from the secret societies. Without the ground work of and the molestations by the secret societies, the God-worshippers might not have advanced so rapidly and extensively as they actually did; without the Taipings the secret society members would still have harassed the Manchus on a less extensive scale, but probably been more chronic and endurable. Thus the secret societies representing rural poverty-stricken peasants and urban unemployed workers and scoundrels, still held the legitimate right of tyrannicide or revolution, as they had many times in Chinese history.

3. The Problem of Ch'ien Chiang and Wang T'ao

Two more problems deserve our attention. The first is Ch'ien Chiang, a romantic character who gave some good advice to the Taiping leaders, who, when his proposal was not accepted, went to the imperial side and is said to have initiated the likin system, a contribution which is now questioned. The other is Wang Wan or Huang Wan, or Wang T'ao, an even more romantic character, who also tendered some golden admonitions to the Taipings as to how to attack Shanghai without disturbing the foreigners and who, when his suggestion was rejected, went over to the government side to offer counterproposals. Later he helped James Legge translate Confucian classics and became one of the most liberal-minded scholars of his time. The lives of these men are full of vicissitudes and problems, and therefore have been the subjects of quite divergent stories.

A. Ch'ien Chiang

(1) His Biography. Ch'ien Chiang (T. Tung-p'ing), a native of Ch'ang-hsing, Chekiang, was a brilliant student who disliked the 'eight-legged' essay and cared little about livelihood. He was fond of wine, boxing, fortunetelling, divination, geography, military tactics, and extensive travel. Romantic and arrogant by nature, he could not stand any restriction and looked down upon everyone in the world. His reputation in his country was bad, and he had no luck in literary examinations, hence was obliged to purchase a bachelor's degree.

Ch'ien went to Kwangtung where Lin Tse-hsü was imperial commissioner to eradicate the opium trade. The outcome was the "Opium War," Lin's banishment, and the foreigners' increased haughtiness. Chagrined at the situation, he assembled the local people and urged the elite to unite the common folk to resist the foreigners. He composed the famous proclamation of warning to exterminate the foreigners (t'ao-i hsi-wen) and led the patriotic people to burn some houses of the British which was a delightful revenge to compensate for humiliation. The local authorities, who were afraid of causing great trouble, arrested him on the ground of agitating the foolish people to injure public affairs. His purchased title was abolished and he was banished to Sinkiang. In exile Ch'ien wrote some beautiful poems expressing nostalgic and patriotic sentiments. He was soon pardoned and returned to Peking where he sojourned for some time.[29]

When the Taipings progressed from Kwangsi to Hunan and Hupeh, Ch'ien is said to have paid a visit to Hung Hsiu-ch'üan to whom he presented a fourteen point policy and a letter advising the Celestial King not to take Szechwan which was hard both to attack and to defend, nor to stay at Wuchang which was too small to maintain the existence of the troops, but to go down along the river and take Nanking as a capital, whence they could conquer the Kiangnan area to secure rich sources of provisions and then to expand to Honan and Shantung. The Heavenly King was too complacent to follow his suggestions. He was made an official in the Taipings and rendered some good service, however.

When Shih Ta-k'ai ran away from the Celestial Capital to take individual action, Ch'ien wrote a letter to stay his trip, strongly reproving him for going to Szechwan. Shih did not take his admonition. Shortly after Shih's departure, Ch'ien also left the Taipings and went to Huai-an and Yangchow, possibly because he anticipated that rebels could not be successful.[30]

When Lei I-hsien, a censor, was entrusted by the emperor with the management of provisions at Yangchow, Ch'ien was invited to work in Lei's camp. At that time (1853) the government force greatly suffered from lack of sufficient funds. In order to relieve the hard-pressed situation Ch'ien offered two policies: to encourage contributions of military funds, and to levy one-thousandth of the value of all goods in transit which was subsequently known as the likin system. Within less than ten days he is said to have raised more than a hundred thousand taels.

Ch'ien became nationally famous on account of his initiation of the likin system, and he was even more arrogant than before. He frequently hurt the feelings of his superior, Lei, by his harsh words. Ch'ien was later beheaded as a result of an argument with Lei. The execution was reported to the emperor as a matter of exigency, because the criminal, Ch'ien Chiang, though a talented man and a fast writer, was not only perverse and insolent, but insurgent. In his autograph prophecy, which was attached to the memorial, he insinuated that the Taipings appeared everywhere and no one could save the situation but him. Were such a dangerous character sent to Peking, he might be intercepted by his comrades and released. Therefore, he was executed immediately in 1853.[31]

Although this story, not a biography, should be received with caution because different sources give various tales, it is an approximate narration of Ch'ien's life.

(2) Does Ch'ien Chiang have any connection with the Taipings and the likin system? According to Kuo T'ing-i's research, in which he collected more material than Hsieh did, it is attested that Ch'ien Chiang had nothing to do with the Taipings whose plan to take Nanking was predetermined in 1851. Nor did Ch'ien have any share in the adoption of the likin system because he joined Lei's camp in April or May 1853

and was killed after twenty days, whereas the _likin_ had already been put into practice. The system was based on copies of old regulations left in various guilds in Hsien-nü chen, Yangchow.[32] Thus neither Ch'ien nor Lei was the originator. That is why a new theory of the origin of _likin_ is claimed.[33] However, it is proper to let experts like Lo Yü-tung and Edwin Beal investigate the question more thoroughly.

We agree with Kuo's conclusion that Ch'ien Chiang had nothing to do with the Taipings' capture of Nanking as their capital. As far as the time element is concerned, only Kuo's evidence to disprove the common conception of Ch'ien as an originator of _likin_ seems to be very weak.

B. Wang T'ao.

(1) The problem. In the spring of 1862 the government force captured a letter signed "Huang Wan, Lan-ch'ing of the Province of Su-fu" presenting to a Taiping leader tactful methods of attacking Shanghai.[34] It has become a question whether Wang Wan, Huang Wan, and Wang T'ao are the same person or not, and whether the letter was written by the owner of one of these names or not.

(2) The principal ideas of Wang's letter. The letter is so important that had the Taipings followed it, their failure might have been turned into success. The author perceived that the purpose of England and France in China was trade, not causing trouble with the Taipings unless their territories were invaded. It was better to maintain amicable relations with them for the time being than to attack them so as to lose foreign help and to incur frontier disturbances. He offered tactful methods by first having the Loyal Prince candidly inform the consul-generals of England and France that if they expelled the Manchu force from Shanghai, Hung Hsiu-ch'üan would be delighted to have trade with them peacefully; if they failed to do so, they would lose their ground. Secondly, Shanghai should not be assaulted suddenly, but the surrounding cities taken, letting the foreigners maintain their expensive guards so long that they would become neglectful and weary. Then the plan was to let the Taipings pretend to live as ordinary people in the city or the suburbs and

set a date to make a raid upon Shanghai from both inside and out.
It would be necessary to cut off the arms and legs and choke its mouth
by occupying Sungkiang, Wusung, and other near-by places, so that the
foreigners would be bottled up and their goods and munitions soon
exhausted. Then the Taipings could collect large amounts of customs
duties to meet the state expenditures. From Shanghai they could re-
cover Anking, Chiu-kiang, and Hankow, make connections again with Shih
Ta-k'ai, and the combined forces could be directed to take the territories south of the Yellow River. After the capture of the commercial
city, Hankow, the foreigners would make peace at Shanghai.

Wang also strongly warned the Taipings to consider Tseng Kuo-
fan's camp at Anking a real danger. He believed it was better for
the time being to put the foreigners aside without any concern, and
to concentrate the Taiping force in the upper valley of the Yangtze
where, when it was pacified after a few years, the foreigners would
naturally bow their heads as subordinates.

This is the idea of Wang's letter. Unfortunately, his farsighted proposals were not accepted by the Taiping leaders. On the
other hand, when the document fell to the government, the imperial
officials were alarmed and great precautional measures were taken.

(3) New strides in the solution of the problem. As a result of
careful independent research by Hsieh Hsing-yao, Chien Yu-wen, and
others, it is agreed that the document was really written by Wang T'ao,
whose handwriting and ideas in later writings can be traced as identical with those expressed in it.[35] His original name was Wang Wan
(T. Li-ping, H. Lan-ch'ing). After being accused of alliance with
the Taipings, he changed his name to Wang T'ao, (T. Tzu-ch'üan, H.
Chung-t'ao),[36] but again changed it to Huang Wan for taboo purpose
He was a native of K'un-shan, not of Ch'ang-chow.

During boyhood Wang was described as frequently sick but
brilliant in study, and he held a hsiu-ts'ai, or bachelor's degree.
By nature he was very proud; he considered no one was his equal.
After the death of his father he went to Shanghai (1849) and worked
in the printing office of Thomas Meadows for fourteen years. He

made the acquaintance of many wellknown scholars. His life was
licentious and immoral.[37]

In 1860 when the Taipings conquered Suchow and Ch'ang-chow,
Wang T'ao was kept at home visiting his ailing mother and he was unable to return to Shanghai. It was during this time that he opened
a small shop and had some dealings with the Taipings. His letter to
them was submitted on January 4, 1862. After it was captured and he
was charged with being a communicator with the rebels, it was ordered
that he be arrested and put in jail. Through the help of his Western
friends, especially T. T. Meadows,[38] he was soon set free. At that
time he was thirty-five years old. Probably it was during this period
that he wrote a long letter to "a certain authority offering them items
to suppress the Taipings and another ten points about using weapons,
training militia, and hiring officers to command Chinese troops."[39]
In the autumn of that year, he was invited by James Legge to serve as
a tutor or assistant in Hongkong. He spent six years in Kwangtung,
making friends with local dignitaries and exchanging poems with Yung
Wing. During that time, the Taipings were defeated and anyone who
had had associations with them was considered a great disgrace.
Therefore, in Wang's writings he tried to whitewash his previous
dealings by taking an antagonistic attitude toward them, and also
by changing all forms of his names.

In the winter of 1867 Wang T'ao was taken by James Legge to
Scotland to help the latter translate Chinese classics into English,
and he took that opportunity to travel in various European countries
where he wrote scholarly and friendly letters in Chinese to eminent
sinologists. After spending twenty-eight months in Europe, he returned with 11,000 volumes of foreign books to Hongkong in 1870[40]
where he lived a miserable and lonely life. In 1873 he was an editor
of a Hongkong newspaper, in 1879 he made a trip to Japan where he
made friends and had correspondence with them, left in his writings.
In 1884 he was the editor-in-chief of the Shen-pao in Shanghai. In
the following year he opened a publishing house using wooden movable
type.[41] The date of Wang T'ao's death is uncertain, one source
putting it at 1890,[42] another at 1897,[43] and a third at 1882.[44]

Probably 1890 is a more accurate date since all his activities ceased a few years before the '90's.

In reading Wang's essays and letters, he impresses us as having been a good scholar, a fluent writer, and a man of talent and far-sightedness who had firsthand knowledge of Europe. But he lacked integrity. Possibly that was because of his selfish ambition to find a good position whether it was with the government or the Taipings. To our surprise we find from his writings that he had given detailed and useful suggestions to the government before Suchow was taken. Thus we may say that Wang T'ao changed sides not twice, but three times, first to the government, then to the Taipings, and then to the government again.[45] Because he wrote a letter to the Taipings, Wang T'ao was charged as being the first candidate or chuang-yüan of the civil service examinations of the long-haired bandits. This charge has been disproved by Hsieh Hsing-yao, Chien Yu-wen, and others.

The three problems discussed in the brief summary above occupy a large and varied amount of literature connected with the Taipings. As a matter of fact, they are not vitally important so far as the history of the whole period is concerned. The extent of literature about these problems is possibly the result of the inclination to record gossip and hearsay, and also exercise the critical spirit created in China after 1919.

IV. THE NATURE, CAUSES, AND EARLY HISTORY OF THE REBELLION

1. <u>Its Nature and Significance</u>

The Taiping movement was an agrarian, racial, and political
revolution.[1] The Taipings were called at the time "Long-haired
bandits" or, briefly, "Hair-bandits" or "the Kwangsi bandits." Since
the revolution of 1911 they have gradually come to be regarded as
revolutionists, and their movement has been generally treated with
sympathy and respect. Now they are esteemed by Hsieh Hsing-yao as
most significant in the history of the Chinese revolution so far as
their national spirit and their attempted reforms are concerned;[2] by
Chien Yu-wen as not only the most important revolution of Chinese history but also of world history with far reaching effects on many facets
of Chinese political, military, economic, cultural, and diplomatic life;[3]
and by Hsiao I-shan as a surging flood of Chinese nationalism which im-
parts the conclusion that there have been many previous attempts and
gives encouragement to the twentieth century revolutionists.[4]

Other scholars with progressive ideas unanimously hail the Taiping
movement, alleging that it was the forerunner of the capitalist-demo-
cratic revolution and the first shot in the republican revolution of 1911;[5]
that it was an anti-feudal revolution coming spontaneously from the minds
of the multitudes of peasant-farmers with far more advanced ideas than
those held near the end of the Ming Dynasty;[6] that it was the general
and total expression of all chronic peasant uprisings in the past[7] and
that it was not a civil war for dynastic change or usurpation of power,
nor was it like the peasant riots led by Huang Ch'ao (d. 884), Li Tzu-
ch'eng (1605?-1643), and Chang Hsien-chung (1605-1647), but a revolutionary war full of nationalistic sentiment to fight against the imperial
and feudal lords. In other words, the revolution of the Heavenly Kingdom
of the Taipings has been given great overtones of anti-feudalism and anti-
imperialism with a view to achieving the emancipation of the oppressed
people.[8] The most explicit explanation of the nature and significance
of the Taiping movement is given by Li Ting-sheng, who perceives the
great revolutionary war as a collective struggle of thousands and
millions of badly "squeezed" peasants against the remaining influence

of feudalism; the movement stirred up not only a nationwide racial war against the rule of the Manchu government, but also an epoch-making agrarian revolution against the feudal monopoly of land. Its aims included the breakdown of the feudalistic land relation between the landlords and tenants, the emancipation of women and the equality of men and women, the abolition of a social system under which the aristocrats oppressed the common people and, finally, the deprivation of the special privileges of the nobility. It was the natural outcome of the combined pressure of foreign capitalism and domestic feudalism.[9]

These are evaluations of the Taiping movement by scholars with some inclination to new historical interpretation. Their analysis may not always be accurate and their conclusions should be accepted with caution, or questioned as is done by Chien Yu-wen. Chien does not think that the Taiping movement is an agrarian revolution, because even though most of the members were peasants, they were also oppressed mainly by Hunan peasants, "How can it be called an agrarian revolution when peasants fight against peasants?" Nor does he consider the Taipings anti-feudal, for even though they attempted to overthrow the Manchu dynasty, they established their own celestial court and restored some feudal practices.[10]

There are also famous scholars in China who still look on the Taipings as ignorant, simple-minded people who carried on a rebellion and tried to destroy all the traditional systems of China.[11]

The majority of opinion, however, including that of many Japanese scholars, is overwhelmingly favorable and sympathetic to the Taipings.[12] In spite of Chien's objection, it seems still to be safe to say that the nature of the Taiping revolution was threefold. It was an agrarian revolution, because the farmers needed a readjustment of land ownership and they had started uprisings toward that goal long before the Taipings' well-organized movement, which at first had been anti-feudalism with a sort of primitive communism, but which later became corrupt. It was a political revolution because the leaders tried to change the government organization and the economic system so that all farmers would have land to till and all men and women would be equal; even foreigners were to be treated on an equal basis with Chinese. It. was a racial revolution to get rid of the Manchu yoke.

The significance of the Taipings was admirably understood as early as 1852 by Dr. Hobson, Bishop of Victoria, who said that "This movement is the most important epoch in the modern history of China, and these occurrences are but ushering in events of almost unparallelled magnitude, and on an almost unexampled scale, for the political, social, moral and religious emancipation of China."[13] Indeed it was the greatest war in human history before World War I, 1914-1918, and it gave the Manchu dynasty a blow from which it never recovered, leaving deep scars in China. In the field of the history of political theory, it was also the first time China had an ideological revolution stimulated by an alien culture or theory.[14] Thus the various points of view concerning the nature and significance of the Taiping rebellion have been presented for digestion and reconsideration.

2. The Causes of the Taiping Rebellion

A. Political Corruption.

The economic cause of the Taiping rebellion has been stressed by Chinese, Japanese, and American scholars. Important as it was, the writer is inclined to think that all revolutions or civil wars in China have been stirred up primarily by political corruption. From political corruption come economic depression, military weakness, foreign aggression, and cultural stagnancy. In short, political corruption is the fundamental cause and it is the source of all evils. With this brief preamble in view, let us analyze the causes of the Taiping revolution.

(1) The Cyclical Theory of Peace and Disorder. In Chinese history there has been a cycle of peace and chaos which was pointed out even as early as Mencius. During time of peace Chinese rulers did not pay too much attention to economic development and the future welfare of the people, and so a period of chaos followed. After turmoil the population was considerably decreased, more land was available for people to work

and they could endure their labor and live comfortably for a while.
This was considered a golden age in the eyes of the Lao-pai-hsing.
Shortly after, however, the population was again increasing daily and
arable land steadily became less available, agricultural methods were
not improved, means of irrigation were not ameliorated, the amount of
production was reduced and the labor increased, and the standard of
living of farmers was lowered. The people did not know the causes and
could do nothing, but burned incense to pray to Buddha or other gods for
a better life. They became fatalists, their fortune depending entirely
upon natural phenomena. Therefore, in China there is a proverb that
in every thirty years there is a small upheaval and in every hundred
years there is a great tumult. In time of famine local bandits arose
like bees and people had no means of making a living. Therefore small
riots turned into great rebellions. After a period of ruthless slaughter
the population was naturally diminished and people desired peace without
regard for any political system or any cost which they had to pay for it.
Thus the cyclical theory of peace and disorder in Chinese history was
formed.

   (2) The Manchu Oppression of the Chinese People. After the Manchu
conquered China, much land and many houses owned by Chinese people were
taken away at will by the Manchus and such usurpations were not entirely
forbidden until the beginning of K'ang-hsi (1662, or to be exact 1666).[15]
So many Chinese farmers were rendered landless. During the Manchu cam-
paigns in South China the conquerors ruthlessly slaughtered thousands
and thousands of people in Kiangsu, Chekiang, Kwangtung. The notorious
Ten days' massacre in Yangchow was merely one of those cruelties which
have been vividly described in a famous book.[16] There were many similar
cases which have not been brought to our attention.[17] Apart from this,
some Chinese scholars were trampled down and some lured by attractive
titles or by lucrative positions and were controlled in their way of
thinking and expression. There were repeated literary persecutions such
as have been admirably expounded by Professor L. C. Goodrich. Therefore,
during the reigns of K'ang-hsi (1662-1722), Yung-cheng (1723-1735), and
Ch'ien-lung (1736-1795) the Manchu dynasty reached its heyday of prosperity and peace. The downtrodden Chinese seem to have been divided into

two levels, the upper and the lower. The upper class seems to have been subdivided again into two. One group was purchased by or yielded to the Manchu rulers and cooperated halfheartedly or wholeheartedly with them. The others, like Huang Tsung-hsi (1610-1695),[18] Ku Yen-wu (1613-1682),[19] Wang Fu-chih (1619-1692),[20] and so on, refused to have anything to do with their enemies, but wrote books to spread the idea of nationalism which were the seeds for later nationalistic movements by the leaders of the Taiping rebellion, the leaders of the reform movement of 1898, and the Kuomintang. The lower class in time of peace enjoyed their farm life, but in time of disorder they organized secret societies, carried on underworld activities, and waited for a ripe opportunity to start a revolution against the Manchu rulers. The fact that Chinese were not allowed to hold important government positions, but were working as slaves, and that the Manchu lords and soldiers had many privileges and held much land enabling them to live very lavishly and idly, were all additional elements to irritate the Chinese and to stimulate their racial conscience.

(3) The Official Squeeze of Public Funds and Mistreatment of the People. Theoretically, after 1711 no increase of land tax was to be permitted for the rest of the dynasty,[21] and the Manchu emperors repeatedly exempted or delayed all taxes in order to win the hearts of the conquered. Practically, however, the Manchus had to resort to other means to raise funds to meet their expenses. In 1674 (not 1649) the sale of literary titles and lower government posts was first adopted by the Manchu ruler.[22] During the reigns of K'ang-hsi and Yung-cheng, when there were military expeditions in the northwest, the same method was used to raise money to make up the deficiency in the national revenue. As time went on more ranks and official posts were purchasable. An ordinary citizen in the morning, after paying 1700 taels of silver, could become a magnificent member of the official class in the evening; if he paid one thousand taels more, he could have priority in being installed in an actual office of magistracy; and if he paid another thousand, he could sit in the chair of a magistrate immediately.[23] So altogether for 3700 taels he could buy a very honorable and powerful position as a magistrate who was supposed to have direct contact with

the people, but because his position had been obtained in this way, he was obliged to extort money or contributions from them. In the whole country many of the financial officers, the governor-generals, and their subordinates of various levels took it for granted that they would get some extra money out of public funds or directly from the people to make up for their insufficient regular salaries.[24] The prevalence of such practice reached a pinnacle near the end of Ch'ien-lung or the eighteenth century when it was said that the Emperor's favorite, Ho-shen (1750-1799), who had held as many as twenty offices at one time, had extracted a wealth of 223,895,160 taels in the treasury and a huge accumulation of jewels, real estate, and so on, before his property was confiscated in 1799.[25] The total value of his property may be established to be eight hundred million taels, a huge sum in eighteenth century China.[26] Naturally, all money accumulated by officials came directly or indirectly out of the pockets of the people who could not make a living but turned into roving beggars and bandits and tried to incite local riots. The local governors, however, usually kept silent, as if there were no such occurrences, because what they desired most was to have nothing happen during their tenure of office, and the "state ministers also hinted saying that flood, drought and bandits were not to be reported in order to save the trouble of the Emperor and save the limited national revenue which was not permitted to be used for such trifles."[27] This account is considered by Hsieh Hsing-yao to be reliable, because the one who wrote it was Lung Ch'i-ju, a native of Kwangsi, who was the first successful chin-shih of 1821 and who secured reliable information about Kwangsi and the policy of the court.[28]

(4) Activities of Secret Societies. Because of the quiescent and laissez-faire policy of local governors who cared for getting money for themselves and finishing their tenure of office, but cared nothing for the welfare of or the riots among the people, room was prepared and opportunity arose for the activities of the secret societies such as the White Lotus, and the T'ien-ti-hui or Triad, whose purpose was primarily anti-Manchu and whose members were mostly poor workers and peasants. As early as 1774 several thousand secret society members attacked Lin-ch'ing in Shantung only to be suppressed by a great Manchu general.[29] In 1781 the Mohammedans in Kansu rebelled against Manchu officials and

were suppressed in six months. Three years later (1784) they revolted again and were temporarily quelled by great Manchu generals.[30] In 1786 the leader of the Heaven and Earth Society, Lin Shuang-wen (d. 1788), started a revolution at Tai-wan or Formosa and fought a bloody war against the Manchu garrisons for a whole year.[31] From 1793-1802 the members of the White Lotus Society started a revolution to extinguish the Manchus and restore the Han, and fought for ten years in an area of five provinces - Hupei, Honan, Szechwan, Shansi, and Kansu, and cost the Manchu court a large sum in war expenses to mobilize the force of the whole empire to wipe out the rebellion.[32] In 1812 the members of the T'ien-li-chiao under the leadership of Lin Ch'ing even attempted a coup d'état in the Peking palace[33] and in 1832 Chao Chin-lung, a man of the Yao stock started another riot in Hunan and was quickly responded to by other Yaos in Kwangtung. The government force had a difficult time dealing with them.[34] These are only a few examples of many insurrections. Although all these attempts were abortive, they never gave up hope of regaining strength to form a larger scale rebellion. They were undoubtedly the forerunners of the Taiping rebellion, the leaders of which must have received much influence and indirect stimulation and encouragement from them, if they were not close allies.

B. Economic Depression.

(1) Annexation of Land by Landowners and Accumulation of Wealth by Merchants. In 1748 the governor of Hunan memorialized, "In recent days about fifty or sixty per cent of land has come into the hands of rich families and those who owned land in former times are now become tenants. Their annual income is insufficient to provide food for the year, and necessarily, to buy rice. But after the harvest the rich families will not sell their grain until they wait for a good price, so actually they control the power of the high and low price of grain."[35] This description was not limited to Hunan but represented the general condition of the whole country. A few years before (1743) a high official requested limitation of holdings of land, saying that each family should not have more than thirty ch'ing or 453.90 acres.[36]

From this we know that there must have been many families who owned more land than that. In 1766 a rich family in Chihli owned more than a hundred and fifty thousand acres.[37] According to a special study in the middle of the nineteenth century from 40 to 80 per cent of the total land of the whole country was concentrated in the hands of 10 to 30 per cent of the people; the majority of 60 to 90 per cent of the people were landless.[38] This rough estimation can give us only a small impression of actual conditions. The really big landlords were usually so powerful that they paid little tax, whereas the poor farmers, besides the regular amount of tax, which was less than that of the Ming dynasty, had to pay three or four times more, illegally charged by the local gentry, the tax collectors, and the local governors. In the middle of the nineteenth century people arose in waves to refuse to pay the land tax.[39] The tax and the extra charges in the provinces along the Yangtze valley were so heavy that various authors agree that it was very necessary to have an agrarian reform and that even if there had been no Hung Hsiu-ch'üan, a revolution would have been inevitable per se.[40]

The merchants liked to hold prices in order to make a big profit. They also lent money to people for exorbitant interest. Consequently, there were quite a number of rich merchants in Peking and other large cities. The owners of pawnshops, which were popular in China, always charged heavy interest also, and these owners were mostly affluent merchants. While the landowners and the businessmen lived a very extravagant and comfortable life, the majority of Chinese farmers had to struggle for existence under a very low standard of living.

(2) Rapid Increase of Population with Disproportionate Increase of Arable Land. According to the Ch'ing-shih-lu in 1751 the population was 181,811,359 and in 1851 it was 432,164,047, the population being more than doubled in a century.[41] It goes without saying that such a statistical figure is not necessarily reliable but it suffices to give us some general impression. As for arable land, the figure available in 1681 was 6,788,843 ch'ing;[42] in 1766 it was increased to 7,414,495 ch'ing.[43] So, over a span of eighty-five years the increase was only 8.5 per cent. It is far less, proportionally, than the increase of

population. As early as 1724 an imperial decree called attention
to the grave situation saying that the population was daily becoming
more numerous and the arable land increased only a little.[44] Though
the population kept increasing, there were not many industrial cities
to absorb it, nor did the Manchu government allow Chinese to emigrate
to Manchuria, Mongolia, and Sinkiang. Therefore, many people were compelled by hard lives to become either salt and opium smugglers, roving
beggars, or bandits. This generally poor condition served as an indirect or remote cause of the Taiping rebellion.

(3) The Outflow of Silver in Exchange for Opium. In the nineteenth century the imports of opium increased year by year and from 1828
to 1835 each year China spent more than thirteen million dollars of
silver on opium. These figures are given in detail by H. B. Morse in The
International Relations of the Chinese Empire.[45] At the same time
China's imports were also greater than her exports. Both the increase of opium and the unbalanced trade became greater and greater
so as to cause a continual outflow of silver and a bad inflation.

Before the nineteenth century a tael of silver was worth about
one thousand cash. In 1835 it jumped to two thousand cash. The medium
of exchange among the people was cash and the amount of tax they had to
pay was fixed in terms of silver, so they were obliged to pay double
what they did before. On the other hand, the income from their labor
was paid in cash. Actually they got only one half of the silver value.[46]
The effects of the drain of silver, analyzed in a special article,[47]
were as follows: (1) the decadence of rural communities where peasants
could not pay taxes and many laid waste to the land resulting in a reduction of half a million ch'ing of arable land so that while in 1812
the total amount was 7,915,251 ch'ing, in 1833 it was 7,375,219 ch'ing;[48]
(2) the depression of business causing bankruptcy of many large shops,
all trade said to have been reduced 50 to 60 per cent; and (3) a great
deficiency of national revenue, the normal annual amount of which was
45,176,121 but which shrank to 38,597,750 in 1841 and to 37,010,019
in 1849 owing chiefly to the shortage of land tax and the paucity of
customs duties due to the smuggling of goods.[49] This grave situation
prepared the way for the operations of the insurgents.

(4) Famine in Successive Years. In time of good harvest Chinese farmers can barely manage to live. In time of famine it is very hard for them to keep their bones and flesh together. Unfortunately from 1826 to 1850 there were frequent floods and droughts in China as is shown in Yao Shan-yu's study.[50] There was a series of natural catastrophes in Honan in 1847 and in the middle of the Yangtze valley in 1849.[51] On the eve of the Taiping revolution there was another great famine in Hunan where many starving people were obliged to fight for the food used to feed the pigs,[52] and in Kwangsi where the governor ordered the troublesome hungry people instantly killed.[53] These conditions motivated many members to join the Taipings.

(5) Continual Riots. There were many local riots inspired either by the poor living conditions or by the members of secret societies and also sometimes the farmers just automatically arose to reject the collection of taxes by the corrupt governors. In any case in the middle of the nineteenth century the uprisings of the Mohammedans, the Miao, and the Nien "bandits" and other local insurgents were very active here and there almost in the whole country. It is not necessary to give a list or a few examples of such insurrections in this little essay since such material is available in many works on the Taiping movement.[54] Suffice it to say that the insurgents in Kwangsi and elsewhere wrote on their white flags "Officials compel people to revolt" or "Heaven is getting tired of the Manchu" or "The Chu family of the Ming is arising again,"[55] which adequately expresses the resentment of the people.

The whole political and economic situation is so ably summarized by Tseng Kuo-fan in a memorial to the Emperor on February 7, 1852, that one can hardly bear to omit much from the translation because each sentence has its value. In the memorial referring to a complete report of the people's distress Tseng says:

"... The virtuous will of the sage emperor cannot reach the people and the distress among the people cannot appeal to the emperor. Your Minister ventures to mention them one by one.

"The first is that the silver price is too high so it is difficult to pay taxes........ In former days a tael of silver

was worth one thousand cash; then a picul [=133 pounds] of
rice could get three taels of silver. Nowadays one tael
of silver is worth two thousand cash and one picul of rice
only gets one tael and a half of silver. In former days to
sell three tou or pecks [1 peck = 1/10 of a picul] of rice
could pay the land tax for one mou [ca. 1/6 of an acre] and
still have something left. Nowadays to sell six tou or
pecks of rice to pay the land tax for one mou is still not
enough. The Court naturally keeps the regular amount of
the annual tax but the small people actually have to pay
twice the tax.... Those who have no power to pay are in-
numerable. The officers in the counties and districts ex-
haust their full strength to urge them to pay...soldiers
and government servants are sent out everywhere pursuing
and compelling them day and night, whipping them all over
the houses and their blood and flesh are spreading in disorder. Are all these actions of cruel officers? No, because if they do not do so, when it is time to check their
achievement they cannot collect 70 per cent of the required
amount and they fear impeachment which usually costs them
thousands of taels and leaves trouble to their descendents.
Therefore, before 1835 the full amount of tax in Kiangsu was
paid. From 1836 to the present(1852) every year is reported
a season of dearth and every year people have to be excused
entirely or delayed from paying taxes.... Therefore, there
is a method of chieh-ch'uan which is an advanced collection
at the time of the spring to levy the tax of the coming
spring, or in this year to check the tax certificate of the
coming year. When the small people do not respond, then
the tax is slightly reduced in order to make them come.
The more advanced the collection is, the larger the deficiency
is. The succeeding official has nothing to collect, so even
a very good functionary has no means to keep his integrity;
for a covetous official, he secures a further pretext for treating the people as his fish and meat.... Since the soaring of
the price of silver, the people's paying of tax becomes more
difficult and the officials urging and reprimanding likewise
become more cruel. Sometimes if the proper family cannot pay,
then the rich members of the same clan are arrested, hand-
cuffed and charged to pay on their behalf. Sometimes they
even handcuff their relatives and imprison their neighbors.
The people hate and resist and so form into big cases of
rioting such as in Lei-yang and Ch'ung-yang of Hunan and Kwangtung, respectively.... It is also caused by the doubling of
the silver price, the extra collection of the tax by officials
and the illegal punishment by government soldiers and servants.
People are really in the condition of being unable to live day
by day. That is one of what your minister calls distress among
the people.

"Secondly, the thieves and bandits are too numerous and it
is difficult for good people to live peacefully.... Recently it

is heard that the bandits' power has become more severe.
They plunder and rape people in the daylight and kidnap
the people for ransom. People cannot help but appeal to the
officials. When the officials go in to arrest, an announcement is proclaimed in advance and till the government (force)
reaches the spot the local gentry usually tell a lie that the
bandits have fled. The officials then burn the people's houses
in the neighborhood for demonstration before they leave, while
the soldiers and the government servants will illegally extract
money and property from the suffering host, and load up fully
before they return, and yet actually the bandits have not fled.
Sometimes it is trickily said that the bandit is killed by
putting another prisoner to death in order to substitute the
case and yet actually the bandit does not die. When the case
of plunder is not cleared up, the lost articles are not returned and the family of the suffering host is already bankrupt, he has to swallow his voice, to sip his own tears and has
no more strength to reappeal. Even if he does, and fortunately
soldiers are dispatched to meet together and to arrest the
bandits, nevertheless the soldiers in ordinary times all have
connections with the bandits and at the very time they will set
the latter free after getting a bribe and leave no footstep to
trace. Sometimes, on the contrary, they take the pretext of
calling them bandits to frighten the foolish villagers and
forcing them to pay a heavy bribery. Otherwise, they will be
accused as collaborators of bandits, their houses will be
burned and they will be tied up with fetters.... Today the
bad soldiers and harmful government employees who foster
bandits and set bandits free appear everywhere. This is another
one of what your minister calls distress among the people.

"The third one is that the unjustified imprisonments are
too many, so it is difficult for people to redress their
grievances.... When one family has a long-pending case ten
families become bankrupt. When one person is falsely charged
a hundred persons will be involved in his suffering. There is
frequently a tiny, small case which is not concluded for years.
The right and wrong are turned upside down and the accused
become old and die in prison which makes one's hair stand on
end upon hearing it. This is again another one of what your
minister calls distress among the people."[56]

This document is very important. It is a summary of summaries from
gazetteers and memorials which were read or handled by Tseng Kuo-fan when
he was a high official in Peking.[57] Every statement he makes can be
verified one by one from the Ch'ing shih-lu or the Tung-hua-lu and all
statements made by Tseng Kuo-fan not only reveal the local conditions
but also uncover nationwide phenomena. Therefore, it is an excellent
presentation of the general background and causes of the Taiping

-46-

rebellion. Based on this document a Chinese Communist scholar, Fan Wen-lan, interprets the second distress by saying that the real bandits were the whole administrative bureaucracy. From the officials down to the soldiers and servants there were none who did not burn people's houses and squeeze people's property and money. Using the arresting of bandits as a pretext they were actually burning, killing, and plundering the people. On the third distress Fan also comments that Chinese law pro-tects corruption and squeeze. Though these interpretations and comments seem to be radical, they are not without ground.

C. The Defeat of the Opium War Indirectly Fosters the Taiping Rebellion.

The defeat of the Opium War revealed the weakness of the Eight Banners. Not only the Manchu troops, but all soldiers of China

> "make connections with bandits as a profession. All are
> smoking opium; all gather together in gambling halls. All
> provinces are like this, and, in general, when nothing
> happens they loaf around with a very arrogant manner.
> When something does happen they hire some helpless persons
> to take their places, who see the bandits in the distance
> and flee and scatter as soon as they see the dust. When
> the bandits run away, the soldiers kill some people to claim
> a victory." 58

This is again a description by Tseng Kuo-fan in 1851. Meanwhile, when China was defeated by England, the Chinese officials and soldiers were very much afraid of the British. General Wu-lan-t ai (d. 1852) says "The army has never recovered from the disorganization caused by the want of success in the 'barbarian affairs,' so that the troops do not attend to order; regard retreat on the eve of battle as 'old custom'; and the abandonment of places they should hold as an 'ordinary affair.'"59 This clearly shows the effect of the "Opium War" on the morale of Chinese soldiers as seen by a brave commander in the battlefield of Kwangsi.

But some Chinese people had different reactions to the foreign aggression. A large group of Cantonese in a village called San-yüan-li gathered several thousand people and attempted to wipe out the British. Another group of Cantonese organized militia at Fu-shan to fight against the invaders. Those Cantonese who had had contact with the foreigners for a long time had a sharper nationalistic consciousness. They were benefited during the early part of the international trade but they suffered a sudden depression during and after the Opium War, when Canton was no longer the sole trading port. Many Cantonese who had worked for foreigners or who transported goods for them were rendered jobless and racial hatred, combined with economic suffering, compelled them to fight hard and madly against the British. The latter did not offer much resistance in order to avoid trouble which was taken by the villagers as a sign that the British were intimidated by the local braves and militia. Thus it gave rise to a proverb, "The people are afraid of officials, the officials are afraid of the foreign devils and the foreign devils are afraid of the people."[60] When the people could frighten those whom even the Chinese officials were afraid of, then how powerful were the people! This is the reason that Karl Marx says the Taiping rebellion was caused by British cannon and that the Opium War actually waked the Chinese people.[61] Whether this is correct or not is better left to the judgement of our readers. It is safe to say, however, that the Opium War had both direct and indirect influence on the rebellion.

In addition to what has been said above, which paints the general background and gives the remote causations, two or three other points may be stated. The first is that the stubborn and adventurous spirit of the Cantonese people may have helped the revolution; those people suffered greatly from the early years of the Manchu regime and they also suffered from their contacts with the red-haired or other devils.[62] Furthermore, through their contacts with the foreigners and missionaries they obtained some new ideas. That is why many reform or revolutionary leaders in nineteenth century China were Cantonese.

Kwangtung is close to Kwangsi which was far from Peking and where the governor, who was especially corrupt, liked to write poetry and to make excursions, but let bandits and other things follow their natural courses. So the Cantonese leaders equipped with some ideas, the pirates harassed by the British naval forces,[63] and the workers who had lost their jobs with foreigners in Canton[64] went to the mountains of Kwangsi where for a number of years there had been a harbor for bandits and the starving and where the local people and the Hakkas or guest settlers who moved in from other parts of China frequently fought against each other.

Finally, but perhaps one of the most important causes, was the religious inspiration of a kind of homemade Christianity created by Hung Hsiu-ch'üan and others who organized the poverty-stricken people to start a revolt against the molesting government troops who interfered with their worship of God. The Taiping rebellion was "the outburst of a religious fanaticism," but as Yung Wing also said, "Neither Christianity nor religious persecution was the immediate and logical cause of the rebellion of 1850."[65] Yung took misgovernment by the Manchu regime as the primary cause. P'eng Tse-i also considers that the religious reform of the Taiping revolution was a secondary cause,[66] the main ones being political and economic. Regardless of whether it is a main or a secondary cause, the religious influence played a very important role in the inspiration, organization, and consolidation of the rebel force. Certainly, it cannot be neglected. Through the fanatic religious inspiration and the attractive slogan, "For Sharing the Property Together," many farmers and poor people were incited to follow the leaders, rolling down like waves along the Yangtze to Nanking. That the rich people could not enter into the kingdom of heaven seemed to fit well the situation of the Taiping followers who were chosen by God through the medium of famine and maladministration.

3. The Early History of the Taiping Rebellion

In recent years several new works have been available on the early history of the movement and some special studies, especially those of Chien Yu-wen, have thrown much light on this part of the history and have corrected many previous errors.

A. The Early History of Hung Hsiu-ch'üan.

The founder of the Taiping Rebellion, Hung Hsiu-ch'üan, was born in 1814 instead of 1813, as is usually given because the date of his birth is the tenth of the twelfth moon of the eighteenth year of Chia-ch'ing, which is January 1, 1814. This new date, which is one out of nine different dates, has been agreed upon by Chien and Lo Erh-kang[67] and is acceptable.

The family name of the Heavenly King was really Hung and his original given name was Fuo-hsiu, Hsiu-ch'üan being the polite title which he adopted after his illness in 1837. This explanation clears up many Chinese documents which have assigned many other family names to Hung.[68] Hung Hsiu-ch'üan was a native of Hua-hsien, Kwangtung, and a son of Hung Ching-yang, not of Kuo-yu as was previously thought.[69] Ching-yang had three sons and two daughters, the eldest of which was Jen-hua, the second Jen-ta, the next a daughter, Hsin-ying, and the Heavenly King was the fourth in the family. The youngest was a daughter, the well-known Hsüan-chiao, wife of the King of the West. The early history of the Hung family goes back to the Sung dynasty when it was in central China. Some few hundred years ago, in order to avoid civil war, the family moved to Canton and so Hung was a Hakka or guest settler.[70]

The guest settlers had much to do with the revolution because they were often cheated by the original residents of Kwangsi and Kwangtung and they frequently had to fight against them for subsistence. They still spoke their own language which was different from the local dialect but closer to the common language. Most of them lived in mountainous areas, working hard for a bare livelihood. Gradually, they were characterized for a firm and strong spirit, brave in fighting and rich in independence and adventurousness. Both the men and the women, simple and naive, were arduous workers who could stand any hardship because they were compelled to do so by their environment. Their women never had their feet bound and their ability to work hard was equal to that of the men. This was also necessitated by their economic environment. They had strong group spirit and organizing power which was another result of their historical environment. After the Manchus conquered China, most of the guest settlers remained un-surrendered for more than twenty years. They had a strong feeling against the Manchus and an equally strong feeling for restoring China to the Chinese. They were full of nationalistic sentiment and revo-lutionary spirit.[71] Not only was the Heavenly King, Hung Hsiu-ch'üan, the descendent of guest settlers, Feng Yün-shan was also a guest settler. Most of their staff members and soldiers came of the same stock, the Hakkas thereby playing an important role in the revolution.

Hung Hsiu-ch'üan was born on a farm surrounded by some four hundred families in the whole village. When he was seven years old he was sent to school and was described as a diligent and bright student with a very good memory. Within a span of five or six years he learned by heart the Four Books, the Five Classics, the Classic of Filial Piety, and many pieces of model essays and poems. During his boyhood he also learned some history and other miscellaneous books.[72] In 1828, when he was sixteen years old, he was obliged to stop studying because of his family's financial straits and from the age of eighteen to thirty-one, that is from 1830 to 1843, he was primarily engaged in being a village schoolteacher.[73] In the meantime, however, Hung might have studied for some time in 1836 under the famous scholar, Chu Tz'u-ch'i (H. Chiu-chiang, 1807-1882), who believed in the evolutionary theory of the three generations of the Kung-yang interpretation of the Spring and Autumn Annals, and the cosmopolitan idea in the Book of Rites, such theories being inherited later on by K'ang Yu-wei (1858-1927) in his reform movement near the end of the nineteenth century. Whether Hung actually studied or listened to some lectures of Chu or not is hard to ascertain. If he did, then it is sufficient to give some background from Hung's education in understanding why he frequently expressed traditional Confucian ideas and high ideals of cosmopolitanism in his later writings.[73]

B. Hung's Failures in the Literary Examinations and A New Interpretation of his Visions.

(1) Failure in examination. From boyhood Hung Hsiu-ch'üan was ambitious, egocentric, and irritable. He liked to be the leader of his playmates who either took his orders or were beaten.[74] He participated many times in the civil service examination in order to be qualified as a member of the Chinese elite which had many privileges. He was successful in a few preliminary examinations, but he failed in the metropolitan examination for the hsiu-ts'ai or bachelor's degree. In 1836, when he was twenty-four years old, he went to Canton to participate in the examination, but he failed. One day while he was walking in the street,

he saw an old foreigner with a long beard with a middle-aged Chinese interpreter at his side preaching the Gospel. Upon approaching them he was given a series of booklets under the general title of Ch'üan-shih liang-yen or "Good Words to Exhort the Age." Many sources say that after Hung received this set of booklets, he put them away without examining them at all, but Chien Yu-wen states that Hung gave the set a cursory examination before putting them aside for many years.[75] Coincidentally, I have had the same opinion. The date on which he received these pamphlets also varies[76] but for the time being we take it to be 1837.

(2) Hung's Illness and Visions. In the following year when he was twenty-five years old he went to Canton to take the metropolitan examination for the third time, but he failed once more. He was so dismayed that like a disappointed lover whose love is turned into hate, or like a poor Peking man, who, walking in a cloud of dust raised by an automobile, curses all automobile-owners and the whole capitalistic system, or like Huang Ch'ao who, failing in the civil service examinations became a great rebel leader devastating the country far and wide, so Hung Hsiu-ch'üan too turned his ambitions in another direction. Hung Hsiu-ch'üan was just a Huang Ch'ao of the nineteenth century.

After this failure, according to his cousin, Hung Jen-kan, Hsiu-ch'üan wrote a poem which reads:

> The dragon hiding in a sea corner fears to
>
> disturb the sky,
>
> He is waiting for the gathering of the wind
>
> and clouds
>
> Before he flies to all directions of the sky
>
> and sets the universe in order[77]

Were this poem true, Hung Hsiu-ch'üan must have had revolutionary and imperial ambitions as early as 1837.

But writing poetry alone could not assuage his great dismay and
bitter disappointment. He was ill and became unconscious. During his
forty days' illness, he had the well-known visions of seeing God the
Father, and Jesus Christ, the Elder Brother.[78]

(3) The Motivation and the Reliability of the Visions. Now let
us ask why Hung was ill for forty days, no more, no less. How reliable
is the story, and if it is reliable, how did it come to pass and become
firmly believed by Hung, himself, and by his followers through the whole
dynasty?

The first question, though no one has asked it before, is easy to
answer because the "forty days" of Jesus Christ's fasting is frequently
mentioned in the Ch'üan-shih liang-yen and so Hung Hsiu-ch'üan was ill
exactly for the same length of time.

The second question about the reliability of Hung's visions was
first raised by Hung Ta-ch'üan who thought that the whole story was
invented by Hung Hsiu-ch'üan and Feng Yun-shan to fool the people.[79]
Since the existence of Hung Ta-ch'üan is still in question, perhaps the
statement he made in prison was edited by Manchu examiners in order to
spoil the reputation and attraction of the rebel chief. But since the
same story is mentioned in five primary sources[80] recorded by Hung
Jen-kan and others who were eye-witnesses, it cannot be utterly ground-
less. The records of the visions, however, differ in detail from one
another. Professor Ku Chieh-kang's theory that historical fictions
are developed like a spiral, the later the date the more complicated
the story,[81] can be applied to Hung's visions, that is, the earlier the
record the more simple, the later ones being complicated to suit revolutionary purposes. The earliest record, Hung Hsiu-ch'üan lai-li,
written in 1852 is very terse, while the latest one, T'ai-p'ing t'ien-jih,
printed in 1862 gives a detailed and systematic story of Hung's inter-
view with God and his discussions with Jesus Christ. In the latter
document, Confucius is arrested and whipped before God, because his
writings, full of errors, have ruined people's minds.[82] This serves as
the basis of the Taipings' cultural policy in revising Confucian classics.

Although the visions were firmly believed by the Taiping leaders

and adherents from the beginning to the end, and had tremendous influence and impact on the whole movement, they were obviously created
for political purposes.

But there was some ground or basis for the story of the visions.
A new light has been thrown on this problem.

(4) A New Interpretation of Hung's Visions. According to Chien's
careful examination, Hung was unconscious or seriously ill for three
or four days, not for forty days successively. Under a high fever
he muttered some unintelligible words and had various kinds of illusions
and visions. A psychologist calls these "visual hallucinations," which
are not entirely fabricated but are recalled from some previous impressions in the mind. Chien Yu-wen is of the opinion that the old
man in Hung's visions was just the old preacher with the long beard
whom he had seen the previous year in a Canton street, while the middle-
aged man was the preacher's assistant. But the later records of the
Taiping considered the old man to be God and the middle-aged man to be
Jesus Christ.[83] This is certainly a very able piece of interpretation.

C. Genesis of the Revolution.

After Hung Hsiu-ch'üan's illness in 1837, he is described as
greatly changed both physically and mentally. He gained some weight
and behaved with dignity as if he were an emperor. He encouraged
people to become gentlemen and reprimanded those who were unprincipled.
He was at the same time still a poor school teacher and he lived a
humble life. This miserable livelihood drove him to put aside his
imperial ambitions for a while and to try once more in the government
civil service examination hoping to be successful and and to become
great through the regular channels. Unfortunately, he failed again
in this fourth and last trial in the metropolitan examination in 1843
when he was thirty-one years of age. His repeated failure was caused
mainly by the corruption of the examination, and was not necessarily
any reflection on his ability to compose the "eight-legged" essays. He
was even more dismayed than at the last failure. He was filled with
anger and hatred and threw all his books on the floor, shouting,
"Wait until we examine scholars of the Empire ourselves."[84] From

this time on Hung was determined to start a revolution to overthrow the Manchu government. It was then shortly after the Opium War and the Supplementary treaty was signed near Canton, the aggressive actions of Cantonese against the British were taking place and Hung saw or heard of all those activities. The Cantonese were robust, active, brave, impressive, straightforward, frank, violent, irritable, emotional, individualistic, adventurous, good in fighting, fond of freedom, full of revolutionary ideas and nationalist spirit. Hung Hsiu-ch'üan had all these characteristics which, combined with his chagrin at his repeated failure at the examinations, made him from that time on anti-Manchu. [85]

The nine booklets under the title Ch'üan-shih liang-yen supplied Hung with new ideas and new inspiration. It was in 1843 that his cousin, Li Ching-fang took out the work and read it, and discovered that there were many wonderful ideas in it. The religious work is generally narrated as having been read "by accident" but it was necessarily so. After the announcement of the treaties with England in 1843, foreigners and foreign books were suddenly respected in a way.[86] That summer he began to preach the Christian doctrine which he got from this work to his family members and villagers. One of his earliest converts was his close school-friend, Feng Yün-shan, who later on became the staunch supporter of his religious and revolutionary movement. The religious ideas in the Ch'üan-shih liang-yen were simple, but many quotations or interpretations from the Bible were so poorly translated and retold that they were easily misunderstood.[87] Many expressions such as T'ien-kuo or the Heavenly Kingdom were mistaken to be China, the chosen people of God were Hung Hsiu-ch'üan and the Chinese, and so on. So Christianity in Hung's mind was merely worshipping of one God, not worshipping any ancestor or idol, belief in Jesus Christ who could redeem one's crimes or sins and help one to be good in the hope that after death the soul could enter Paradise and enjoy permanent happiness. The religious ceremonies and practices consisted mainly of destroying idols including Confucian tablets and Catholic images, of writing the name of God on a piece of paper, kneeling before it as usual, burning incense, lighting candles, offering

wine and sacrificial dishes in worshipping Him. After several months
the paper tablet was deemed improper and was discarded and they bowed
and kowtowed to the sky. Such religious ideas were combined with Hung's
revolutionary movement.

As a result of the joint efforts of Chien and Lo, it has been decided that it was in the year 1844 that Hung Hsiu-ch'üan lost his job
as schoolteacher on account of destroying Confucian tablets, and he was
unable to live in his native district. He and his close associate Feng
Yün-shan had to run away without a definite destination at first.
They travelled in vain in Canton and in several other large cities
around the provincial capital to find a suitable place to start a
revolution. Then they decided to go to Kwangsi to join one of Hung's
cousins by the name of Wang Sheng-chün,[88] who lived in a village
called Tz'u-ku-ts'un about fifty <u>li</u> to the northeast of Kuei-hsien.
They stayed at that place from April to July and then Hung realized
that it was a good place to preach the Gospel but not good enough to
become the base of a revolution. Moreover Wang was not rich and could
not support them, so they went back to Canton rather disappointedly.
But during their stay in that village they made more than a hundred
converts.

In 1845, Hung Hsiu-ch'üan again made a living by tutoring pupils
at home and it was during this year that he wrote two articles, the
<u>Yüan-tao chiu-shih-ko</u> and the <u>Yüan-tao hsing-shih-hsün</u> which represented
Hung's ideas of that time. Basically, they were Confucian, but a little
Christian thought was superimposed. In the following year he wrote
three more essays, one was <u>Yüan-tao chüeh-shih-hsün</u> in which he attacked
the "Yen-lo-yao" or the Devil-king of Hell and made obeisance to the
Shang-ti or God who created the universe and myriad objects in six days.
He also quoted Chinese historical facts from ancient times down to his
own to persuade people not to worship idols. A second essay was <u>Pai-
cheng-ko</u>, a song of a hundred correct things to do, expressing his
moral conception of standing in awe before God, behaving well, cultiva-
ting virtue and other Confucian thoughts. The third essay is lost.
In 1847 he and his cousin, Hung Jen-kan went to Canton to study the
Bible under the Reverend I. J. Roberts, a Baptist missionary from

Tennessee,[89] under whom Hung spent about two months reading the Bible and receiving some real instruction. He was very much liked by Roberts because of his educational background, but two other assistants of Roberts were jealous lest he take their places, and so they advised him to request to be baptised and to be paid one tael and a half per month as a stipend. Roberts did not like "rice Christians,"[90] and refused to baptise him, so Hung ran away without any grudge and did not realize the trick of his colleagues until later years.

While Hung Hsiu-ch'üan stayed in Canton writing books as the kernel of his religious and revolutionary theory, Feng Yün-shan remained in Kwangsi doing hard labor to make a living and going from place to place in order to make more converts and to find more revolutionary comrades. It was Feng who organized the "Pai-shang-ti-hui" or the Association of God-worshippers and wrote all the regulations for this society. It was also Feng who selected the real base, Tzu-chin-shan, "Thistlemount," about fifty li north of Kuei-p'ing, Kwangsi, as the headquarters of the rebellion. Thus, while Hung Hsiu-ch'üan was the theoretical leader, Feng Yün-shan was the real manager and actual planner of the revolution. For a period of six years, from 1843 to 1849, both Feng and Hung suffered a great deal from their poor living and all kinds of difficulties, but their strong determination overcame all obstacles. In July 1847 Hung Hsiu-ch'üan joined Feng Yün-shan at "Thistlemount" where the Association of God-worshippers was systematically organized and where there were more than three thousand members. They had heard the name of Hung Hsiu-ch'üan for a long time, and they immediately welcomed him as their leader. The two men cooperated to enlarge their influence in the neighboring districts, and they attracted poor farmers and workers at first, and later on even some powerful local gentry, who joined them with all of their followers.[91]

D. The Basic Staff of the Taiping Rebellion.

During the preparatory period of the revolution, 1843-1849, Hung and Feng persuaded many able members to join them and to become the basic staff in their movement. The origin of the following persons may be briefly mentioned:

Yang Hsiu-ch'ing (d. September 2, 1856), a man of little or no education, a charcoal worker near the "Thistlemount in Kuei-p'ing

was the most cunning of the Taipings and later on became the number
two head, the commander-in-chief, and the prime minister of the
Taiping state. When he was very young he was left bereft of his parents
and was homeless. According to <u>Tsei-ching hui-tsuan</u> (ch. I) he was one
of the transporters of foreign goods and associated with many itinerants
between Kwangtung and Kwangsi. After the Treaty of Nanking he lost his
job, and went home to become a charcoal worker again. This information,
however, is not supported by modern research students. When he joined
the Taipings he was thirty-odd years old. Partly because of his personal
ability and partly because of his position as a maternal uncle of a
superior and patron of Hung and Feng, Yang soon became a leading figure
among the rebels.[92] He was full of plans, good in military affairs and
expert in commanding and controlling people and spying out the secrets
of enemies as well as those of his comrades. He was the first person
who discovered the visions of Hung Hsiu-ch'üan who had revelations of
God. In March 1848, Yang claimed also to be a communicator of the
will of God. Hung was obliged to accede to his authority.

In September another leader, Hsiao Ch'ao-kuei (d. 1852), brother-
in-law of Hung, a farmer and native of Wu-hsüan claimed to be a communicator of the will of Jesus Christ, and Hung acknowledged it to be true.
Hsiao was a sworn brother of Yang and was also a woodcutter. After the
start of the revolution, he was made Western King, while Yang was made
the Eastern King, and his position was inferior to that of Yang but
superior to that of Feng.

Why did Yang and Hsiao claim to have revelations of God and Jesus
Christ, and why did Hung approve their practice? According to studies
of recent years, it was a common practice of some magicians, who could
hypnotize themselves, to imitate the voice of some dead person and to
talk of things in the past and predict the future like fortunetellers.
The local people firmly believed in them. Such superstition is still
prevalent in Kwangsi and Hunan. When Hung Hsiu-ch'üan was away and
Feng Yün-shan was in prison on account of destroying idols in temples
(1847-48), the followers began to lose faith. It was at that time that
both Yang and Hsiao claimed to have such authority, to give orders on
behalf of God and Jesus Christ, respectively, in order to consolidate
the beliefs of their followers. For political reasons and for pro-
tecting his own secret in order to defend his divine right, Hung had

-58-

to admit the truth of their having such power, but that sowed the seeds of later internal struggle.[93]

Another Taiping leader was Wei Ch'ang-hui (original name Wei Cheng, d. 1856), a Hakka land and pawnshop owner of Chin-t'ien village and an educated man, who had experience in transacting business with local officials. During the great famine of 1849, he gave much grain and money for famine relief and so secured a large number of supporters. He led the members of his whole clan to join the insurgents. In Chien Yu-wen's field investigation he has collected much information about Wei's person and his family history.[94]

Shih Ta-k'ai (1821-1863), a guest settler of Kuei-hsien, was formerly believed to be the best educated man among the Taipings and to be excellent in both military and literary affairs, but in his own statement from prison he said that during boyhood he had studied without much achievement and so took farming as his profession. He did not have any literary degree in contrast to traditional claims, although he studied for some time. He was a rich farmer of the district and he contributed a large part of the provisions for the early movement of the Taipings. Many of his poems and essays have proved to be forgeries. Both Lo and Chien believe that he was born in 1831, not 1821, joining the Taipings when he was twenty years old and already parentless. Therefore, the traditional account that his parents were killed at Nanking during the internal struggle is not true.[95]

As for their original followers, several thousand of them were Hakka farmers, a few hundred were charcoal workers, about one thousand were miners, and the large majority were peasants. There were also among the adherents of Wei Ch'ang-hui merchants and radicals as well as a few rich farmers and well-educated people. There were many members of secret societies, mutinous soldiers from the government side, and also a number of porters of Kwangtung. According to Yung Wing there were more than ten thousand porters and convoys who carried foreign goods from Canton overland to Siangtan, Hunan. After the shifting of the trade center many unemployed workers were attracted by the Taipings. Wu Ju-hsiao, an interpreter for foreign merchants in Canton, went to Kwangsi and became a leader.[96] Altogether there were some thirty thousand basic members at the beginning of the revolution.[97] They were very well organized, strictly disciplined with iron rules and enthusiastically inspired by their religious ideas under the command of Hung, Yang, Feng, Hsiao, Wei, Shih, and others.

E. The Start of the Revolution.

The date of the revolution varies according to different sources. Some put it in the sixth, the eighth, the ninth, the eleventh moon, and so forth, of 1850. Many Western and Japanese sources consider June 1850 as the beginning of the rebellion.[98] According to Chien Yu-wen the month of June was the time when a general order was issued to have the members concentrate at Chin-t'ien. The actual date of the start of the revolution was on the tenth of the twelfth moon which was the thirty-eighth birthday of Hung Hsiu-ch'üan. After a celebration, a flag was formally raised at the ancestral temple of Wei Ch'ang-hui to start the revolution. The tenth of the twelfth moon was January 1, 1851, and this date is agreed to by Lo Erh-kang.[99] Both authors reached this conclusion after careful research, and it should be accepted.

V. NEW LIGHT ON THE MILITARY DEVELOPMENT
1. The Victorious Period from 1851 to 1856

The destruction of idols and temples caused animosity among the local gentry. The clash between the God-worshippers and the militia of local gentry became so severe that a large scale rebellion developed and the government force was mobilized to fight against them. All God-worshippers were ordered to withstand the government troops, to follow their chiefs to any destination without thought of their families. Their homes were destroyed and all movable property was delivered to a general treasury from which they shared alike. The prospect of sharing all property in common inspired thousands of poor guest settlers and tenants to join the reform.

After the inauguration of the revolution at the beginning of 1851, Hung was unanimously declared the T'ien-wang, "Celestial King," of the Taiping T'ien-kuo, "Celestial Kingdom of Peace," and the year 1851 was

the first year of the new dynasty.[1] It was at this time that most of
the political and social systems were formed. The old statement that
Hung declared himself emperor and adopted the title for the nation only
after he took Yung-an on September 25, 1851, is considered erroneous by
Chien Yu-wen.[2]

At Yung-an the Taipings were beseiged by the government forces from
the winter of 1851 to April 6, 1852, when they escaped the siege. The
questionable figure, Hung Ta-ch'üan, was captured at this time and was
later executed at Peking. The Taipings fled from Yung-an to Kuei-lin,
capital of Kwangsi, and then to Ch'üan-chow (June 3). Their able leader,
Feng Yün-shan, was killed near that place in June 1852. The loss of this
loyal, brave and talented leader is considered by Chien Yu-wen the beginning of Taiping decline, because during this battle many well disciplined
soldiers and officers were lost and the new recruits were inferior in
discipline and order, and the sharp spirit of the army was diminished.[3]

After reorganization the Taipings renewed their campaign from Hunan
to Hupei and finally they took Nanking on March 19, 1853, after a short
siege of eleven days. It took only twenty-seven months to cover the
large area from Kwangsi to Nanking. During the war the Manchu troops
mainly relied on the protection of the thick walls and big cannon, whereas
the Taipings resorted to brave assaults and to tunnels dug under the city
walls by miners.

After the Taipings took Nanking, they established it as their capital.
Hung Hsiu-ch'üan dispatched one expedition to North China with the purpose of capturing Peking. This northern expedition reached the vicinity
of Tientsin, whereupon the Manchu court was so frightened that Emperor
Wen-tsung ordered in advance that the tributes of provincial authorities
should be sent to him in Jehol since Peking would soon be lost.[4] Their
panic in the palace was even greater than that during the Boxer Uprising
in 1900.[5] If this expedition had been better prepared, new materials
from various sources indicate that Peking could have been taken easily,
and the Taipings could then have conquered the whole of China. Unfortunately, communication lines were not well maintained, cavalry was non-
existent, and the southerners were not used to the northern diet nor
prepared for severe cold weather. Consequently, they were finally suppressed

by the famous Mongolian general, Seng-ko-lin-ch'in (d. 1865) in 1855.
Because no Western source mentions anything about the northern expedition, Hsieh Hsing-yao and Chien Yu-wen have each written a detailed
account of it.[6] Unhappily, there is not enough space to give a summary
of these military actions in this pamphlet.

Another expedition was sent westward to retake Kiangsi, Anhwei,
Hupei, and Hunan, which the Taipings had once rapidly passed through,
like the later German blitzkrieg, without leaving garrisons, and as a
result these provinces had to be reconquered. Unluckily, a strong
opponent, Tseng Kuo-fan, organized a kind of Confusian religious army
to fight against Hung's pseudo-Christian army, thereby developing a
war of ideology, or of Chinese culture against alien culture. Being
a pure scholar, Tseng was at first badly harassed by the Taipings.
His newly trained "Hunan Braves" suffered many defeats, and his newly
organized "navy" was well-nigh annihilated (February 1854), at which
time Tseng was so humiliated that he attempted to commit suicide by
jumping into the water, only to be dragged out by his subordinates.
Afterward, he was badly harassed again in 1856 by the almost invincible
Taiping leader, Shih Ta-k'ai, at Nanchang. At the same time the
Manchu force under the command of Hsiang Jung (d. 1856), which pursued
the Taipings from Kwangsi to Nanking and encamped there for many
years, was crushed. Such military developments are succintly summarized in Tseng Kuo-fan's biography in the Eminent Chinese of the
Ch'ing Period.

2. Reasons for the Victories

A. Effective Ideology.

Ideology is the most powerful weapon in political movements. The
Taiping ideology was a strange combination of religious, political,
and racial elements. Starting with a few Christian ideas: that duty
to God is supreme; that all idols of Buddhism, Taoism, and all ancestral
and Confucian tablets should be destroyed; that opium-smoking, gambling,
and adultery should be prohibited; the Taiping leaders gradually
directed their adherents from pure God-worshipping and iconoclasm to includ

-62-

corrupt officials, the gentry, and soldiers among the evil devil-spirits who should be destroyed or overthrown. Thus a naive religious movement was quickly shifted to a political movement for the overthrow of the corrupt officials, the tyrannical government, and the Manchu dynasty. The three elements, religious, political, and racial were thus interwoven into one logical unit. God's second son, Hung Hsiu-ch'üan, was the real divine emperor who led a righteous army to render China unto the Chinese and to bring paradise on earth so that all the children of God could enjoy peace and prosperity. Such ideology played an important role in inspiring Taiping adherents to give up their farms, houses, and property and join the Taipings zealously with their whole families. The enthusiastic adherents were also well commanded by several able leaders in the early days of the revolution, and they fought overwhelmingly against the aimless, mercenary, government force.[7]

   B. Solid Organization.

   At the inception of the movement, the Taipings were well organized on a military basis patterned after the military system of the Chou-li or the Book of Rites, and the militia organization of Ch'i Chi-kuang (d.ca.1586) of the Ming dynasty.[8] Their official record, T'ai-p'ing chün-mu,[9] tells us the details of organization. Without taking the trouble to present a series of military terms and their scale of official ranks, we may say that their military organization had two good points. One is the unified command and the other is elastic organization. The Heavenly King was theoretically the top military chief under whom there was a post of commander-in-chief held by Yang Hsiu-ch'ing; under Yang there were a deputy commander-in-chief, Feng Yün-shan, and two associate deputy commanders-in-chief, Wei Ch'ang-hui and Shih Ta-k'ai. The five kings were each concurrently the commanding general of an army. Each king had individual responsibility and used his own ingenuity to deal with enemies as a matter of exigency, but at the same time there was close cooperation and concentration of command and planning. Though the commanders had different ranks, they could work at the same time as a committee to plan their strategy very carefully. Under a sole supreme command there was military efficiency, and under a committee plan there was over-all vigilance. This kind of organization was applied to a small force of twenty or thirty thousand men at the commencement of the rebellion and also to a much larger force in the later period since it was very elastic. The commander was able to order his troops as the mind orders the arms and fingers. In addition they had marvellous group spirit and close cooperation. The commanders were congenial, old friends; the officers and soldiers were mostly guest settlers of Kwangtung and Kwangsi who were famous for their solid, group spirit in fighting against their enemies. They were further consolidated and disciplined by a weekly religious service, pre-meal grace, and the ten commandments. Friendship, harmony, cooperation, and mutual help prevailed among the troops. A foreign observer noted that, "The general appearance of the whole force was that of a mob,...but while no discernibl steps were taken for preserving order among them, they all appeared on the best terms with each other; and although engaged in the exciting work of the division of plunder, or of accommodation, no instance of fighting, dispute, or drunkenness came under our observation, nor did we see any of them indulging either in gambling or in smoking tobacco."[10] This was their condition in 1861. They were better in the early years, or at least they behaved much better than the government soldiers. The wives and children accompanied the men in the army and, though strictly separated from seeing each other, served as a mutual guarantee of loyalty to the Taipings and also as encouragement for one another. Therefore, the early Taipings usually fought well.

The government troops were particularly merciless to the rebels of Kwangsi, because they were die-hards, usually preferring death to surrender.[11] Because of the solid organization and strong group spirit, the rebels were superior to the imperialists whose generals were un-cooperative, jealous, and on bad terms with one another, and whose soldiers were timid and spiritless, but troublesome and cruel to the people.[12] Callery and Yvan ironically state: "A Chinese army on a campaign treats friends and enemies with most perfect impartiality, plundering all alike."[13] This is a great understatement.

C. Strict Discipline.

The good organization and group spirit were maintained and fostered by strict discipline. There were sixty-two articles of military law[14] and in the T'ai-p'ing t'iao-kuei[15] there were ten essential rules governing military camps and another ten rules concerning military expeditions. The officers and soldiers were obliged to (1) observe the heavenly rules including religious ceremonies, Sunday services, praying, and singing, (2) obey orders, (3) be harmonious and cooperative, (4) be absolutely loyal - capital punishment was to be given to those who communicated with the enemy, changed sides, or deserted, (5) be brave in fighting, (6) act with integrity - keep no private property and turn everything over to public ownership, (7) get rid of bad habits such as opium and tobacco smoking, drinking wine, gambling, laziness, graft, and superstition, (8) be familiar with the regulations governing military camps and operations such as how to advance, withdraw, attack, defend, get up, call the role, participate in military drill, march in the army and keep order and so on, and (10) observe protocol such as proper address and salute of officers. This is in contrast to the government troops who were undisciplined and disorderly.

D. Good Strategy.

Some Taiping leaders were born strategists. Their military techniques caused modern Chinese communists to make special studies of them.[16] They always selected and advanced to the spots where the resistance was the weakest. They knew how to avoid or by-pass a strong defense and to assault a weak spot such as leaving the well-defended Kuei-lin behind to attack Ch'üan-chow and abandoning the strongly guarded Changsha to advance on Yochow. They knew how to make a detour in order to attack the rear or flank of the enemy's position, and how to confuse the enemy by attacking at one point to divert his attention while actually advancing on another city. They knew how to throw fire torches to burn boats or camps and how to dig tunnels under city walls, and also how to plant mines.[17] They knew how to carry on an offensive war for defensive purposes. They knew how to spy on their enemies, and the activities of their fifth columnists usually preceded a formal military operation. They also knew how to make use of superstitions to render the bodies of their soldiers invulnerable to bullets and how to intoxicate their fighters with strong, medical liquor so that they ran onto the battlefield like mad dogs.[18] In short, good strategy along with their well-disciplined troops counted quite a bit in their rapid success.

E. Favorable Circumstances.

The above four points are internal or subjective reasons. On the external or objective side, the corrupt Manchu political and military machinery from the central to local levels, the prevalence of famine and bandits, the desire to recapture China for the Chinese, the activities of secret societies, the over-population on limited arable land, the unproportional distribution of land, and the distress of poor peoples' lives were, as has been said before, excellent background for smoothing the way for the Taiping victories.

Comparing the strength and weakness of the two sides, Yao Ying (1785-1853), a contemporary government official on the Kwangsi front, made the following remark: "Unanimity of mind, familiarity with geographical conditions and greatness of courage are the enemies' strong points and our weak points. The sharpness of weapons, the abundance of provisions, and the numerousness of soldiers are our strength, but their shortcomings."[19]

This is a keen and accurate observation. The Taipings were reported by foreign observers to have no regular uniforms. "They were mostly armed with long spears and swords, few comparatively having matchlocks."[20] Another observer says, "All the rebel soldiers that we saw were badly armed, the universal weapon being a long bamboo with a pike on the top -- a very small proportion having old muskets, matchlocks, or pistols; a few, fowling-pieces and rifles."[21] Despite poorer equipment, like the early Chinese communists, their better morale, discipline, and organization assisted them in overcoming their shortcomings.

3. The Declining Period, 1856-1864

Unfortunately, the Taipings did not long maintain their advantageous position of 1856. After continued victories, the commander-in-chief, Yang Hsiu-ch'ing, became very ambitious. The result was the following occurrence which was fatal to the aspirations of the insurgents.

A. Internal Dissension, 1856.

A special study of this incident is made by Lo Erh-kang.[22] The root of the matter went back to 1848 when Yang Hsiu-ch'ing claimed that God came into his body to give orders. As pointed out above, it was at that time a political means to bolster the faith of the mob while both Hung and Feng were absent from the God-worshippers. Again for political reasons Hung was obliged to acknowledge Yang's privilege of proclaiming God's orders through his mouth. At the beginning of St. John, chapter III, of the Taiping Bible Hung made an autographic note saying that Yang was a beloved son of God and that he and Yang had been borne by the same sage mother. Thus the Heavenly King and the East King had about equal positions before God. Sometimes he had to kneel before Yang while the latter issued orders on behalf of God or even to receive whipping without hesitation. According to Lo, before the capture of Yung-an on September 25, 1851, the Heavenly King was the real commander-in-chief; but after the capture of Yung-an, the power to issue orders as the real commander-in-chief fell into the hands of Yang Hsiu-ch'ing. When the latter reported military orders to the Heavenly King, he did nothing but approve them. Yang became more arrogant day by day, and We Ch'ang-hui, whose position was only next to Yang's, was very jealous and he hated Yang deeply. The nature of the Heavenly King was very stubborn, irritable, and violent; he compared himself with fire. He could not bear the aggressiveness and humiliation of Yang too long. Nevertheless, after May 1858, when General Hsiang Jung's force, a constant threat outside Nanking, was removed, Yan Hsiu-ching took the opportunity to usurp the throne. Hung on the one hand purposely enhanced Yang's position and gave him the prerogative of being addressed as Wan-sui, "Live for Ten Thousand Years," or "Long Live the Emperor;" on the other hand Hung summoned Wei to the capital to kill Yang.[23]

The great slaughter took place on September 2, 1856, which was thereafter a memorial day to Yang's ascension to heaven. Not only was Yang killed by Wei Ch'ang-hui, but some twenty to thirty thousand of Yang's adherents, soldiers, and family members were also massacred, the whole process taking three months. This event is described in detail by E. C. Bridgeman, North China Herald, No. 366, January 3, 1857, page 91, and by J. Macgowan in the same paper, No. 354, May 9, 1857, page 163. Canny and three others saw the whole tragedy and so they could supply material for a detailed account which coincided with contemporary Chinese records.[24]

Shih Ta-k'ai, who came back to Nanking in September, blamed Wei for his cruelty. Wei was angered and planned to kill Shih. The latter quickly escaped from the city wall after only staying for several hours. He returned to his military camp in Anking. It was then reported that all Shih's family-members, including his parents, in Nanking were killed, but that is not true. New material, mentioned above, shows that Shih's parents died long before. His wife and children, however, were killed in the Celestial Capital.

Through the request of Shih Ta-k'ai, the haughty Wei and the two hundred members of his party were also killed by Hung Hsiu-ch'üan after two days of fighting.

Shih returned to Nanking again, but the Heavenly King was jealous of his popularity, would not entrust him with much administrative power, and, instead, used his two incapable and unpopular brothers, Hung Jen-fa and Jen-ta, in pivotal positions. The two new dignitaries caused trouble with Shih very often. Shih was obliged to leave Nanking in the summer of 1857 and thereafter he launched an independent expedition from Chekiang to Kiangsi, Fukien, Hunan, and Kiangsu, until his death in Szechwan in 1863. Shih Ta-k'ai was a believer in individual heroism. His independent development has been criticized by a modern historian.[25]

B. The Defensive War, 1856-1864.

The Taipings were weakened first by the usurper, Yang, secondly by the bloodthirsty Wei and thirdly, by Hung, who trusted no one but his family members. After 1856 the Taipings lost their spirit. They took the defensive instead of the offensive. They were able to survive for six more years owing to the fact that the successive famines supplied them with inexhaustible soldiers and that two new heroes, Li Hsiu-ch'eng (d. 1864) and Ch'en Yü-ch'eng (d. 1862, aged 26), came into prominence. Li fought in the area east of Nanking and Ch'en, west of the Capital. The two fought hard against the government force, disregarding the corrupt Celestial Court.

Three months after the internal dissension, the Hunan Braves took the offensive and after four years the Taipings were expelled from the provinces of Kiangsi and Hupeh.

From 1860 on the Hunan Braves attacked Anking while the Green Units advanced on Nanking. Li Hsiu-ch'eng adopted brilliant tactics in taking Hangchow by severing the supply line to the government force encamped near the Capital.[26] While the government force was diverted to the rescue of Hangchow, he rapidly sent troops to attack the re-organized force encamped near Nanking and completely routed them on May 6, 1860, thus removing the menace to Nanking. A little new light on this campaign may interest Taiping experts.[27]

Taking this advantageous opportunity, Li Hsiu-ch'eng attacked Shanghai for the first time from May to July 1860, and again in May 1861. (In 1853 and 1855 Shanghai had been occupied by Liu Li-ch'uan's Triads, who had no direct connection with the Nanking Taipings). The two Shanghai expeditions were fruitless and instead incited the foreigners and the rich local merchants to organize troops to fight against them, which later developed into the so-called Ever Victorious Army under Generals Ward, Gordon, and others.

The defense of Anking by Ch'en Yü-ch'eng was broken in August 1861 and Ch'en died at Luchow, Anhwei, 1862. That left Li Hsiu-ch'eng alone to deal with the enemies.[28] From 1861 to 1864 Li fought bravely for the existence of the Taiping cause. He had to resist the general attack of the Hunan Braves under the leadership of Tseng Kuo-fan, the Huai Army under the command of Li Hung-chang, and the Ever Victorious Army which was nominally also under Li's control, but which actually, according to Hsieh Hsing-yao, received orders from the British minister in China. The troops led by foreigners were a great headache to the famous diplomat Li Hung-chang.[29] Despite the combined attack of the government forces, Li managed to prolong the life of the Taiping Dynasty for a few years and made many victories such as the capture of Hangchow in December 1861 and the defeat of the allied forces of Ward and Li Hung-chang at T'ai-ts'ang, May 21, 1862, and so forth. Finally, however, Nanking was taken on July 19, 1864, after a siege of more than two years.

Hung Hsiu-ch'üan committed suicide on the second of June (1864), as one source indicates, and Li Hsiu-ch'eng was executed on the seventh of August. The Taiping Revolution had turned into a complete failure. The credit for suppressing the Taiping Rebellion, which was formerly given to the Ever Victorious Army, now is given to Tseng Kuo-fan. Tseng was a great scholar, thoroughly trained in the eight-legged essays and neo-Confucianism. He was considered the George Washington of China and his famous sayings and his spirit in managing public affairs have served not only as a model for young Chinese students, but also as a guide for General Chiang Kai-shek. Recently, however, he has been accused by radical writers of being a "butcher" and a "traitor" because he was merciless to his enemies and loyal to the Manchu dynasty. It is true that he was cruel to the Taipings, and it is also true that he fought for the Manchus instead of the Chinese. On the other hand he was campaigning for traditional Chinese civilization and so he fought for indigenous Confucianism against an alien Christianity. Although most liberal-minded writers condemn Tseng Kuo-fan very severely, due respect is still generally given to his scholarship and integrity.

The contribution of the Ever Victorious Army is still recognized by Chinese writers, but is not considered of primary importance, as formerly. Most modern Chinese writers consider the Imperialistic or Anglo-French intervention as one of the causes of the failure of the Taipings.

4. Reasons for the Failure of the Taipings

Various facts have been adduced as reasons for the failure of the Taipings by different authors. Chien Yu-wen cites (1) the ineffectiveness of their revolutionary ideology, (2) the disintegration of their basic force, (3) the corruption of the whole Taiping body from high down to low ranks, (4) the errors in strategy and the lack of men of ability, and (5) the assistance rendered to the Manchus by the imperialists.[30] In Yang Sung's analysis, the causes enumerated are (1) the internal struggle of 1856, (2) the creation of ninety-odd feudal kings each maintaining an army and so destroying the unification of military power, and (3) the deterioration of the integrity of officers and morale of soldiers so as to cause trouble to the people and lose their support and cooperation.[31]

A. Political Corruption, the Fundamental Cause.

We believe that political corruption was the fundamental cause of the failure of the Taipings. After Nanking was conquered, the leaders began to live extravagant, indolent, and licentious lives, with a harem of women, contrary to the avowed platform of monogamy. Hung lived as a Taoist emperor who was not bothered either by state affairs or by foreign dignitaries. Since the top-ranking official of the Nanking government acted in such a way, other leaders followed and the morale and discipline of the army also degenerated sharply. Were Hung Hsiu-ch'üan not corrupt, himself, and had he maintained his integrity and exemplary leadership, the mutual slaughter in the internal strife might have been averted, and his religious and political theories might have been fully carried out.

B. The Taipings Reconquered by Chinese Traditions, Provincialism, Familism, and Nepotism.

At the inception of the movement, the Taiping leaders intended to carry on a social revolution against the Chinese superstitions and traditions. Later on factions arose. The Kwangsi faction led by Yang Hsiu-ch'ing oppressed the Kwangtung faction headed by Hung Hsiu-ch'üan.[32] The old members, consisting mostly of people from Kwangtung and Kwangsi, oppressed the new members from Hunan, Hupei, and the natives of the lower valley of the Yangtze. The old members held higher positions than the new ones, and even though they did no actual work, they frequently received rewards from the Heavenly King. The affect on the morale of the new members was such that it caused many of them to go over to the Hunan Braves and the Huai Army later on. The military men were above the intellectuals, who were addressed as Hsien-sheng, and assigned to do clerical or secretarial work.[33] Furthermore, the two able generals, Li Hsiu-ch'eng and Ch'en Yü-ch'eng fought separately and did not inform one another of the grave military situation or extend any aid. The Heavenly King was also not on good terms with Ch'en and Li. As a matter of fact, as noted above, after the internal struggle, he trusted nobody but his family members. Apart from his brothers and cousins, Hung trusted only Cantonese to guard the city of Nanking and hold the keys to all the gates.[34] So familism, provincialism, and nepotism played an important role in the downfall of the Taipings.

Also, most of the Taiping leaders, from Hung on down, imitated the extravagant life of Chinese emperors.[35] Thus one of the motives of Hung's revolution was imperial ambition and one of the causes of failure was also imperial ambition. Each Taiping leader wished to be an emperor. In other words, the Taiping leaders, themselves, became feudalists.

The Taipings were reconquered by Chinese tradition, which can be used as a measure of success or failure in any reform or revolutionary movement in China at the present or in the future.

While the Taipings were thus gradually losing their revolutionary spirit and returning to Chinese tradition, the government side made great progress. The Green Units were replaced by the newly trained Hunan Braves and the Huai Army, who were better paid, disciplined, and equipped, and, therefore, had stronger fighting power than the rebels. Formerly, the loyalists had had neither a good commander-in-chief nor cooperation among the generals. Now they had Tseng-Kuo-fan, who was a farsighted over-all commander who planned everything carefully in advance and to whom all officers, most of whom were directly or indirectly his students, were so loyal that they only recognized him as their superior and did not pay much attention to the Manchu emperor. This marks a turning point in Chinese military history. Before the Taipings, troops were controlled by the court; after the Taipings, troops belonged to individuals.[36] From Tseng Kuo-fan to Li Hung-chang, Yuan Shih-k'ai, and others, the geneology of war lords can be traced from generation to generation. In this respect we may say that Tseng Kuo-fan was the first or ancestor of modern war lords.

C. Lack of Good Leadership and Men of Ability.

Taiping leaders like Hung, Yang, Shih, and Li were limited in number, in education and in caliber. Even of this limited number, most of them died or killed themselves, and after 1857 only a few remained. If their leaders had been good, the Taipings still could have carried on their political and social reforms and made much progress as in the earlier period. Many political and military mistakes could have been avoided and modifications and new inaugurations of policy could have been introduced to suit the needs of the times. Unfortunately, Hung Hsiu-ch'üan was stubborn and narrow-minded, and other leaders had the same inclinations. They could not take advice from others. The proposals offered by Wang T'ao and Yung Wing,[37] to say nothing of Ch'ien Chiang whose connection with the Taipings was dubious, were rejected and those well-educated people later on served the Manchu government.

Not only did the Taipings lack good leadership but they also lacked good men of ability as staff members of military officers. Most of them were illiterate. A man who could read and write was a rare thing in the troops.[38] Because of this dearth of knowledge and education, their policies could hardly be carried through uniformly among their troops, and that impaired the efficiency and effect of their ideas. The lack of good leadership is also a cardinal trouble of modern China.

D. Taiping Ideology Distasteful to the Chinese Gentry Class.

The Taiping ideology, a combination of Christian, Confucian, and Taoist ideas intermingled with some attempt at a primitive Communism and some intention of abolishing Chinese traditions and superstitions, was theoretically not bad at all, but actually it was so advanced that their platforms have not yet been entirely carried into effect in the last century. Unhappily, because the ideology was not carried out by able leaders and by the numerous capable staff members required for propaganda, it was in return described by Tseng Kuo-fan and others as a horrible and distasteful thing against Confucianism and Chinese native civilization so that all the intelligentsia and all the gentry class hated the Taipings and eventually suppressed them. It is as if an ideology were introduced to replace democracy and Christianity in America and England. Objection would be stirred up from the majority of the people. That is also the reason for the failure of the Taiping ideology in China. Some writers feel that the lack of an activated proletarian class at the time of the Taipings was the cause of their downfall.[39] We are of the opinion that the ideology was too advanced for the Chinese people at large to accept, and that their poor leaders did not observe it consistently and could not carry it through effectively.

E. Strategic Mistakes and Foreign Intervention.

The general criticisms of the strategic mistakes are as follows: (1) After Nanking was taken, the Taipings should have concentrated their power to take Peking. Then the center of gravity of the Manchu dynasty would have been lost and the attitude of foreigners would have been changed. (2) They should not have attacked Shanghai in 1860 and 1862, because the purpose of that assault was to protect Nanking and before the attack, both Chinese merchants and the foreigners had no intention of causing trouble at Nanking. Since Shanghai was attacked and the foreign powers had gained new privileges from the treaties of 1858 and 1860, and also because of the exaggerated government propaganda about the severe prohibition of opium and suspension of trade by the Taipings, there was great concern among the profit-seeking merchants. Therefore, the rich foreign businessmen and diplomats in Shanghai organized a military force and rendered financial and military help to the Manchu government to suppress the insurgents. Other minor strategic mistakes need not be mentioned one by one. It is sufficient to know that the above two big errors and foreign intervention constituted one cause of failure.

Apart from the five points mentioned above, the lack of provisions, good weapons, and a naval force are additional causes. However, these minor deficiencies could have been made up by able leaders.

VI. NEW LIGHT ON THE TAIPING RELIGION AND CALENDAR

1. The Taiping Religion

The Taiping religion has aroused much attention from the beginning of the movement down to the present day, because of its connection with Christianity and its combination with local religions. Almost all Western writers paid some attention to the Taiping religion, but none considered it real or pure Christianity. One Chinese author charged another one to have misunderstood the Taipings as Catholics, and, accordingly, wrote a special article to prove that they were Protestants.[1] Eugene Boardman wrote a doctorate thesis on The Biblical

<u>Influence Upon the Ideology of the Taiping Rebellion</u> in which he care-
fully examined the Taiping documents published in 1851-1854 since,
by the end of that time, the original religious purposes of the movement
had already petered out. He compared the Taiping documents with the
Chinese Bible available at that time, and found that the Taiping religion
drew elements from both parts of the Protestant Bible. From the Old Testament came the concept of God as the only God, the supreme creator, and
its corollary that no idols could be worshipped. This God, like Jahweh,
was a personal diety who could be appealed to without the help of a priest.
From the New Testament came the doctrine that God was the God of all men,
not just of the Jews or the Chinese. He was also their Heavenly Father.
His son, Jesus, the Savior (and the Elder Brother of Hung Hsiu-ch'üan),
had been sent down into the world to suffer for the sins of mankind and
to give his life in redemption. The Holy Ghost and the Trinity were
used as names in the ritual, but were not understood. Thus Hung took
the Hebrew idea of God in both the Old and New Testaments, the illustra-
tive stories of the Pentateuch, the Ten Commandments, the Old Testament
attitudes toward the worship of idols and rival gods, the Biblical ideas
of Satan and Evil spirits, and of heaven and earth, the basic facts of
Christ's life, the teachings of Christ, and the Christian rites and
doctrine. Hung failed to echo the Christian emphasis on the forces of
love and concern for one's neighbor. The Christian virtue of humility
was completely overlooked, and the important sacrament of the Lord's
Supper was neglected.[2]

On the whole, Eugene Boardman has done a solid piece of work. Since
he is indefatigably revising the introductory and concluding chapters,
it is improper to summarize too much of its contents. It is hoped that
the work may be published soon.

Now, without giving an unnecessary precis of the opinion of other
writers one by one, let us discuss the Taiping religion as follows:

A. The Sources of Christian Knowledge of the Taiping Leaders.

Hung Hsiu-ch'üan secured his Christian knowledge from the nine
tracts, <u>Ch'üan-shih liang-yen</u>, of which the original English title is
"Good Words to Admonish the Age," and from about two months training
with an American missionary, I. J. Roberts. Other early Taiping leaders

got their Christian knowledge from Hung.

The Ch'üan-shih liang-yen consists of nine books, altogether 235 leaves and about 90,000 words, which is less than one-tenth of the quantity of the Chinese Bible. The usual statement that the nine books contained more quotations from the Old Testament than from the New Testament is not true.[3] After an actual examination of the Ch'üan-shih liang-yen, it is found that there are fourteen occasions including fifty-three verses which are quoted from the Old Testament, whereas there are forty-eight occasions including twenty-one chapters and seventy-eight verses where the New Testament is quoted.[4] It is, therefore, very clear that more quotations are made from the New than the Old. The mistake comes from the fact that there are probably not many people who have read the nine little books.[5] Yet the books are so important that as McNe says, "In that moment a set of Liang A-fa's tracts nearly turned China upside down."[6]

The translations were probably done very poorly by the Reverend Charles Gutzloff and Robert Morrison, and the quotations are the same as those in the edition of the Chinese Bible printed by Ying-hua shu-yuan in 1827. The quality is so poor that in many cases they are not comprehensible.[7] The sermons and essays were written or compiled by Liang Fa or Ah-fa (Leang Afah, 1789-1855, one of the earliest Protestant converts of Dr. Milne at the College at Malacca). The whole series was printed at Canton in 1832. The main written source of Christian know-ledge of the Taipings, supplied by Liang, was very meager and sketchy and some of the ideas were even inaccurate because Leang Afah's writing was influenced by a Buddhist monk from Yunnan who almost converted Liang to Buddhism. The ideas of destruction of idols and the torture in hell were repeatedly over-emphasized. Many terms in these nine books were adopted in the government publications of the Taipings. Neverthe-less, some practices of the rebels, such as the new trinity, the observa-tion of the Sabbath, and so forth, were not mentioned in the nine tracts. How much Hung Hsiu-ch'üan learned from Roberts during his two-month sojou with him is still a field open for further research.

B. The Incomplete and Inaccurate Imitation of Christian Practices.

Well then, how "Christianized" were the Taipings? In brief,
they believed in God, Christ, the atonement, the destruction of idols,
the setting apart of one day, Saturday instead of Sunday, for prayer,
the implicit obedience to the tenets of the Ten Commandments, a grace
before meals, chanting of simple hymns during worship, and a kind of
baptism. In addition, they placed bowls of various kinds of food as
offerings to the Supreme Being, among which were three bowls of tea
or wine, one for each person of the Trinity. They had no church,
however, and no Christian teachers or ministers. Two other leaders
besides Hung Hsiu-ch'üan claimed to have direct revelations and constant personal guidance from God and Jesus Christ. They also had many
other practices which were neither mentioned in the nine tracts nor
in the Holy Bible.

Although Hung Hsiu-ch'üan had never been baptized, the Taiping
creed was his personal religion. He made himself inferior only to
God and Jesus, and superior to the Pope and the King of England.[8]
His superiority complex turned many of his Western brethren into
enemies. His religion was a political religion, a conglomeration of
Christianity, Confucianism, Buddhism, Taoism, superstitions, and
even some Judaism.[9] He was anti-Catholic, and even had one Jesuit
killed.[10] He was friendly to Protestants, but was reluctant to let
them travel in the interior of China unless they obeyed Chinese law.[11]
So Hung's religion also had a sense of nationalism.

C. Influence of Local Religions and Superstitions upon the Taiping
Leaders.

It seems to us that Hung Hsiu-ch'üan and a few other Taiping leaders
were opportunists and shrewd revolutionists. Hung made use of all
religions and superstitions available to achieve his political and
personal ambitions. His visions of and connection with the Christian
God are virtually the same as Han Shan-tung's connection with the
rebirth of the Mi-lo Buddha to inspire a revolution against the Mongol
conqueror. Since China was defeated by England in the Opium War and
the English believed in Christianity, Hung's clinging to God rather
than Buddha would be more attractive and have more influence on the
common people. Hung was clever, not only because he could learn Chinese

classics, but because he could perceive quickly the significance of the Opium War, and the prestige of the victorious foreigners and their religion which made them strong.

Hung Hsiu-ch'üan was perhaps influenced more by local religions, especially Confucianism and Taoism, than by Christianity. Although Hung claimed to be a worshipper of God and to proscribe equally Confucianism, Buddhism, and Taoism, yet the ideas of these three religions were also freely adopted. While on the one hand, at the beginning of the revolutionary movement, he was responsible for the destruction of the Confucian tablets, on the other, he quoted heavily from the Confucian classics, especially those sentences including the term Shang-ti, for his God.[12]   Confucian proverbs or mottoes were quoted as the words of God or Jesus,[13] the Confucian ideas of filial piety, loyalty, and obedience were emphasized in his writings, and the Confucian funeral ceremonies were first adopted for funeral services.[14] While the destruction of idols was carried out from the beginning to the end of the Taiping regime, the Confucian temples were spared,[15] possibly because of the strong objection from the intelligentsia. The Taiping military and land system was mainly influenced by the Confucian classic, The Rites of Chou. Therefore, Thomas Meadows found the Christianity of the Taipings was modified by Confucianism.[16] and Callery and Yvan also considered the insurgents still Confucianists.[17]

From Buddhism and Taoism, the Taipings apparently adopted the ideas of the thirty-three heavens, the eighteen hells, the severe torture in hell, the endless transformation of life, the belief in fatalism, the wish for longevity or immortality, the "Father of Nine Thousand Years," "Seven Thousand Years," and so on. They also stressed the offering of a sacrifice of rice, wine, fowls and pigs to God on such occasions as birthdays, weddings, new construction, the piling up of stones, the digging of earth, the building of kitchen stoves, or on the day when a baby was one month old.[18] They worshiped the spirit of wind, offered sacrifices of good dishes to God, burned written prayers for repentance, selected beautiful girls for the palace from Sunday service, and so forth, all of which was not only contradictory to the Christian spirit, but anti-Christian. They were blasphemies.[19] They were even so superstitious as to believe in the magic power of Taoists who boasted of being able to swallow a knife, vomit fire, and to render their bodies invulnerable to bullets.[20]

After Hung Hsiu-ch'üan reached Nanking, he was a typical Taoist emperor. He never appeared in public, nor did he bother himself much with foreign visitors. He said nothing, but his policy was carried through. He did nothing, but he thought everything would be done. He had a good time and enjoyed himself in his newly-constructed palace with his harem filled with beautiful women, while monogamy was supposed to be the only legal marriage.[21]

D. Use of the Religious Force by the Taiping Leaders.

Although the biblical influence on the Taiping leaders was very limited, misinterpreted, and mixed with local superstitions, basic ideas such as iconoclasm, keeping Sabbath service, and observing the Ten Commandments, and saying grace before eating, were obstinately held throughout most of the years of their government.[22] Their religious ideas were used as the foundation of their theocratic government. They were used to organize, train, and encourage soldiers, to promote hard labor, to prevent soldiers' escape from camp, to check mutiny, and to popularize education. The religious politics stimulated the rise of the Taipings, consolidated their development, maintained their life and also partially caused their fall.[23] Consequently, even though rebel soldiers were cruel, they were on the whole better trained and behaved than the government forces. Even Tseng Kuo-fan was deeply impressed by the fact that when "Nanking was taken, not one of more than a hundred thousand bandits surrendered; they gathered together to burn themselves to death without regret."[24] In this respect the Taipings' religious force was very successful with their soldiers. The T'ien-ch'ing tao-li shu or "The Doctrine of the Love of Heaven" (1854) is an excellent piece of propaganda literature utilizing simple Christian thought to strengthen the belief of soldiers. Thus Christianity, even though in limited fashion had some influence.

E. The Taiping Leaders had Great Creative Powers.

The destruction of idols and burning of Confucian classics helped the Taipings to get away from traditional ideas and to inaugurate new political and social institutions. During the rebellion many old books were burned, many Sung editions were sold by the catty,[25] and Confucian tablets were destroyed. In spite of the fact that this provoked the Confucian scholars to fight against them as a religious army, the Taipings were able to introduce many new political and social ideas which had far-reaching influence on Dr. Sun Yat-sen's revolution in 1912 and on the Communist revolution of the present time. The Taiping leaders suffered from having little education, but because of this they could carry on a bold war against Chinese traditionalism.

2. The Taiping Calendar

Like their religion, the Taiping calendar was nominally a drastic change from lunar to solar. Actually it was neither lunar nor solar, neither Chinese nor Western, but a conglomeration of a little of everything. It was enforced in south China for some fourteen years, and it is a very important instrument for the study of history to straighten out the dates of this period.

According to Tung Tso-pin, an expert on various calendars, a Taiping year was divided into three hundred and sixty-six days and twelve months, of which the odd ones had thirty-one days and the even ones thirty days. Every forty years thirty days were to be subtracted, making each month twenty-eight days and each festival fourteen days. The indication of the year, month, and the day by cyclical signs was based on an old Chinese almanac, and that of the twenty-four solar terms, weekdays, and Sundays was derived from both Western and Chinese almanacs, since, through Mohammedan influence, the Chinese almanac had marked weekdays from the time of the T'ang dynasty.[26] As a result of discussions by correspondence between Tung Tso-pin and Lo Erh-kang, many questions have been answered.

A. When was the Taiping calendar made?

According to Chien Yu-wen,[27] it was made during Feng Yün-shan's imprisonment in Kuei-p'ing in 1847-48, but was not used until 1852. The consensus of opinion of Hsieh Hsing-yao,[28] Kuo T'ing-i,[29] Lo, and Tung is that the calendar was made after October 1851, and put into effect at the beginning of 1852.

B. Who was the maker?

Chien attributes the making of the calendar to Feng Yün-shan,[30] Tung to Yang Hsiu-ch'ing,[31] Lo to Hung Hsiu-ch'üan.[32] Later on, Hung Jen-kan improved it a little. There is no agreement of opinion about the originator yet. Whether it was made by one person or by a few in cooperation, is a question of lesser importance for further research. We are inclined to think that it was a cooperative effort, because in the preface of the 1853 calendar it is clearly stated that "your minister_s_" (plural) made the calendar.

C. Which Concordance of the Taiping Calendar with Chinese and Western Calendars is more reliable?

There are two kinds of concordance: the one is developed from S. Tanaka's list[33] into Hsieh Hsing-yao's chart,[34] and the other is Kuo T'ing-i's table. The latter is more reliable, because Kuo has noticed that the Taiping calendar is one day ahead of Chinese and Western calendars. For instance, Saturday in the Taiping calendar was Sunday in the West. However, neither of these two concordances can be discarded entirely. Tung's advice is that for convenience of historical study, it is best to use Hsieh's chart for dates before February 12, 1853, and after February 13, to consult Kuo's table.[35] Note that the Taiping calendar appended to the popular concordance compiled by Cheng Ho-sheng[36] is based on Hsieh Hsing-yao's chart.

A new study of the Taiping calendar has been made by Lo Erh-kang and published in the magazine Hsüeh-yüan, vol. II, no. 6, pp. 39-62, in which is presented a great deal of new evidence to confirm his former study and to prove Tanaka's list unreliable. In addition, he points out that the dates used by W. H. Medhurst are also wrong. Thus, Kuo T'ing-i's chart seems to be the most reliable for the Taiping history.

D. Why is there one day difference, and when does it begin?

On this point Tung and Lo had prolonged discussions. Kuo considers the one-day difference to have been purposely made to confuse the enemy in order to keep military secrets, and Lo thinks that Hung intentionally made everything different from the Ch'ing system. Both of these explanations are doubted by Tung.[37] After an exchange of notes, the reason for the one-day difference was shifted to the commencement of the calendar. Lo maintains that it began from the

31st of December or January 1, 1852, when the calendar was first enforced. At that time the war was in progress, and there was no celebration on either side, and so from the beginning a mistake was made
unconsciously. The conclusion has been disinclinedly consented to by
Tung.[38]

E. What is the significance of the Taiping Calendar?

The Taiping calendar signifies a revolutionary attempt to replace
the Chinese old almanac which had been in vogue for hundreds of years.
It was a harbinger of the innovation of the Western calendar in the
Republican period. Although it was far from perfect, it was close to
an ideal system for the Chinese farmers as well as the intellectuals.

VII. NEW LIGHT ON TAIPING POLITICAL AND SOCIAL SYSTEMS

The Taiping political and social systems are traced by Hsieh Hsing-y
to three sources: (1) their land distribution and political and military
organizations were derived from the Chou-li; (2) their religious and socia
policies were copied from the Old and New Testaments; (3) their actions ar
habits were mostly influenced by Chinese secret societies.[1]

This analysis is correct in the main. But it is dubious whether
their religious and social policies are entirely copied from the Bible,
because, as we have seen, their Biblical knowledge was very limited and
inaccurate.

There is not much new information on the Taiping political and socia
systems. One small new idea, however, is that these systems were formed
during their occupation of Yung-an, but before that time the leader had
claimed to be king and adopted a dynasty title.[2] Their preparatory work
seems to have been sufficient because at that time Feng Yün-shan, and
Yang Hsiu-ch'ing were on good terms and in close cooperation with Hung
Hsiu-ch'üan. Therefore, they worked out some good new systems.

1. Political System

The Taiping government was theocratic, the Celestial King being
both the spiritual and temporal ruler. Under the Celestial King, there
were five other kings who were both civil and military chiefs and who

acted in council with the leader. Below the kings were marquises, state ministers (Chêng-hsiang), supervisors (Chien-tien), commanders (Chih-hui), generals (Chiang-chün), and so on. Their civil and military organizations were alike, and both resembled ancient Chinese models modified by the leaders' study of some parts of the Testaments. Soldiers were at the same time supposed to be farmers, so the military organization was also social organization. Thus we may say that the Taiping political, military, and social organizations were identical.

The smallest unit was the family. Every twenty-five families formed a larger unit and among these twenty-five families there was a public treasury and a church. All civil and military affairs were conducted by two officers called ssu-ma who worked also as quasi-pastors, teachers, and judges. If there were disputes the two parties first went to the two ssu-ma, the latter listened to the complaints and if their adjustments were not obeyed, the two officers brought the two parties to their imme- diate superiors called the t'su-chang. If the quarrel could not be settled by these officers, then the case was brought step by step to higher officers and finally to the Heavenly King, if necessary, who would make the final decision. Not only judicial affairs, but social affairs were directed by the two ssu-ma. All expenditures of weddings or celebrations of the birth of new babies after one month were drawn from the public treasury, and the amount was limited and universal through- out the whole empire. Marriage was not to be arranged in terms of money and sacrifices were to be offered to God at the wedding ceremony and on other auspicious occasions. Superstitions were not indicated on the calendar, children among the twenty-five families were supposed to attend a church service, where the two ssu-ma taught them to read the Old and New Testaments, and some decrees of the Heavenly King. Boys and girls were to be separated in the church. The work of making pottery, bricks, and tiles and of building houses was supplied by military officers and was done after the harvest. This may be considered their basic political and social organization.[3]

Officers were recruited by civil service examinations which were held once every year to fill vacancies. The system was divided into local, district, county, provincial, and capital examinations. There were military and civil examinations held separately. Various degrees were granted to successful candidates, but the titles were slightly different from the government system, that is, the Hsiu-t'sai or Bachelor's was changed to Hsiu-shih, and so on.[4] The successful candidates were assigned duties. If the new officers were well selected, the examiners would receive a reward. Otherwise they would be punished. The examination themes were frequently taken from the Bible or concerned theological and state affairs. The essays were very poor, stereotyped, and eulogistic.[5] Due to constant warfare examinations were not carried on regularly once a year. Nevertheless, they were given several times.

2. Economic System

The Taipings had a very attractive economic system, a type of primitive communism which is described in detail in the book, T'ien-ch'ao t'ien-mou chih-tu, which is one of the most important documents of the rebels. According to this work, the land was divided into nine grades and was to be equally distributed among the people. There was no distinction between men and women, but the number of people in each family was taken as the basis for receiving land. The more heads, the more land. If there were six persons in one family, three of them were allotted good land, three bad land; the good and bad had to be half and half. The method of receiving land was that every person, regardless of being man or woman, from the age of sixteen and above, received some land and below fifteen, only one-half. If a person over sixteen years old received one mou of good land, then the one below fifteen received only half a mou.

Aside from farming each person was required to have a minor profession, such as the women doing weaving and making clothes, and raising chickens and pigs. People were allowed to take only the amount from the harvest necessary for their subsistence. The rest was forbidden from private ownership, and was to be kept in the public treasury. All agricultural by-products, cloth, chickens, ducks, money, and silver were divided in the same way. No one was permitted to keep any private property, and even the land allotted to him was not to be regarded by the farmer as his personal estate. "All land of the Empire is to be planted together by all people of the Empire. If the land of this place is insufficient, then the land in other parts is assigned." If there were a famine in one part, then the products of other parts where there was a better harvest would be transported to relieve the famine. The purpose was that the great blessings of the Heavenly Father and Heavenly King were to be shared by the people of the whole Empire. Land should be worked by all people, food should be consumed, clothes should be worn, and money should be used by all. There was to be no area which did not equally profit and no person who was not well fed and clothed, because the Empire was a large family of the Heavenly Father and the Heavenly King. If no person of the Empire possessed any private property and all things were turned over to the Lord, the Lord would know how to make use of them, and all people in the Empire would be equal everywhere and would be kept satiated and warm.[6] It was a reflection of the overpopulation and the problem of unequal distribution in the mind of Hung Hsiu-ch'üan, who was born on a farm. This was the plan of their land and communistic system. The basic principle and chief aim was for the abolition of private ownership.

There is a question as to whether this system was put into practice or not. According to foreign observers such as Brine, the Taipings had some modified system of taxation. The farmers in villages had to pay a certain sum varying according to the tenure and grade of land. "The rebel authorities pay a visit to the rural districts once a month, and exact a tribute of cash or rice from the inhabitants of the villages. Regularly-appointed officers are stationed in all important places, in whom the people seem to have confidence."[7] This seems to indicate that the land system was not put into practice. Otherwise, there would have been no land tax. The tax, however, was light and the people were not compelled to pay the full amount of the reduced rate. According to Li Hsiu-ch'eng, "The required land tax of the people of Suchow was by no means completely collected, and the people were allowed to figure out and report on their acre of land and were not deeply pressed."[8] This is a true statement, because it can be proved by the discovery of a certificate which reads:

"Now based on the report of the tax of the landowner
Chou Chih-chi to be 14.8 _mou_, this is the evidence."[9]

This indicates that the Taipings still recognized the position
of landlords and let them report on their own estates. In Chekiang
the land tax of the people and the customs duties of all passes in all
districts were very little in order to assuage peoples' hardships.[10]
That is why the government also tried to reduce the land tax along
the Yangtze in a struggle with the rebels to win the peoples' hearts.[11]

On the other hand, however, the Taiping land system and social
organization may have been put into practice in some parts of the
territory under their jurisdiction for a short time. For instance,
"at Woo-hoo the houses were divided according to a kind of barrack
system."[12] This shows the practice of the local social organizations. Lord Elgin observed in 1854 that "the system of public
granaries and the community of goods sufficiently account for the
almost entire absence of shops and trade."[13] It also signifies that
public treasuries and community of goods were put into practice.
According to Lo Erh-kang, after the Taipings took Nanking, the local
government of counties and districts was organized under the military
system and their communistic ideas were enforced for a while before
1856. After that time, in consideration of the strong objection
from the people, it was abolished. But Lo thinks that the public
ownership system was pushed through in the army by Hung Hsiu-ch'üan
without hesitation. All booty gathered by officers and soldiers during
their attacks on cities was forced to be turned over to the public
granaries, so that no one had any private property. All wealth belonged to the public and was owned and shared by everyone.[14] In short,
the Taiping land system is believed by many Taiping historians to have
never been put into any large scale practice, because the proportional
distribution of land with a reliable census was a very complicated
procedure and the insecurity on the farms caused by continued warfare made it impossible to essay the new system.[15]

3. The Position of Women

The position of women under the Taipings was greatly enhanced.
They were allowed to participate in civil service examinations and to

hold equal civil and military positions with men. There were women
soldiers and women's barracks which antedated the modern WACs.
Foot-binding and prostitution were forbidden and monogamy was promoted.
Woman was recognized by the Taipings in her proper sphere as the com-
panion of man. Education and development of a girl's mind were equally
stressed. Institutions for unprotected women were presided over by
duly appointed matrons and were particularly organized and designed to
educate and protect the young girls who lost their natural guardians or
those married woman whose husbands were away on public duty and who had
no relatives to protect and support them.[16] "In times of danger the
females were placed in positions of safety, as far as possible, and
guarded from all improper intrusions; and this was consistent with their
custom of punishing with death the brutal crimes against women to which
they are usually exposed in the storming of cities."[17] Whether these
descriptions by foreigners were polite expressions on paper or courtesy
for a certain period deserves further investigation.

Marriage under the Taiping regime was compulsory for all classes
of women, and was generally a love-match, not a pecuniary arrangement.[18]
According to Lin-le, "Even in a case where a chief's daughter is given
to some powerful leader compulsion is never used, and the affianced
are given every opportunity to become acquainted with each other."[19]
Except for the wedding ring, a wedding ceremony similar to that of the
Western church was adopted. This was perhaps limited to the time when
the Taipings enjoyed victory. Later on, because of the lack of food
to feed women in the camps, they were compelled to go out of Nanking to
cut rice plants and still later on they were compelled to marry anyone
to whom they were assigned. Some women committed suicide because of
the undesired husbands. Monogamy was the rule for the common people,
but the leaders like Hung Hsiu-ch'üan, Yang Hsiu-ch'ing, and others were
said to have many wives or concubines.

Slavery was totally abolished and the abolition was made effective
by punishment with decapitation.[20]

4. Other Drastic Changes

The destruction of idols and temples was carried on almost through the last years of the dynasty. The use of opium and even of tobacco and alcohol was forbidden. The question is how thoroughly or severely were these prohibitions carried out. According to foreign observers such as Wolseley, "Although smoking is said to be punishable by death, all the officials who visited us were delighted to get cigars," and also "To say that the Tien-wanists deserve any praise for their proclaimed laws prohibiting the use of opium is absurd."[21] Other foreign observers also reported that some Taiping sailors in their ships of war still smoked opium and had special means to buy and to smoke it. Most of the sailors were Cantonese. In the capital and in the army, however, those opium-smokers were to receive death penalties. Foreigners did see several opium offenders actually executed. They also saw several criminals guilty of idolatry receive capital punishment.[22]

From the above citations and other sources which need not be mentioned one by one, it seems safe to say that in the earlier period and in the places where the Taiping authorities played an important part, opium was strictly forbidden in actuality as well as on paper.

5. The Evaluation of the Taiping Political and Social Systems

After briefly examining the various systems mentioned above, let us introduce a few authors who give evaluations of the reform. The first writer is Cahill, who wrote in A Yankee Adventurer, "... under the Taiping control taxation was less burdensome for the villagers and farmers than under Manchu rule, while on the other hand their products were purchased at fair prices and not taken from them forcibly. Apart from strictly enforcing the religious and moral precepts of their faith, overturning idols and temples, and forbidding the use of opium and alcohol, the insurgents did all they could to encourage agriculture and trade. The statistics for these years show that the export of tea actually increased under the Taipings from 1858 to 1862, while silk held its own."[23] This shows that some good effect was achieved.

Another writer, Hsiao Kung-ch'üan, an authority on the history
of Chinese political thought, considers that the contribution of the
Taipings was mostly on the negative side. Their positive contribution
to political thought was after all very limited. This was probably
because their political background was derived from underworld activities
and secret societies. They were just one of the religious-inspired
insurrections like the Yellow Turbans of the Eastern Han and the
White Lotus of the Yüan. Their leaders lacked deep understanding of
Chinese original civilization and Western Christianity. Their ideology
was an agglomeration of miscellaneous things which "is not sufficient to
be a foundation for building up a modern, rich and strong nation."
The essential points of political thought of the Taiping rebellion were
three: First, to revolt against the Ch'ing and to restore the Han.
Hung's nationalistic idea involved two meanings - nationalistic autonomy
and international equality. Secondly, to worship God and to promote
universal love. These are two things worth noticing among their religious
ideas. One is that Hung, Yang, and others recognized that the people were
equal with the ruler before God and the other is that they recognized that
the authority of God not only reached the ministers and the people, but
also controlled the Heavenly King, himself. This fully indicates their
theocracy. The author perceives that the Taiping leaders absorbed universal love from Christianity and developed this idea into universal
brotherhood and the abolition of hatred between one locality and another,
and one country and another. The Empire as a big family in which people
should enjoy peace and own land equally was probably the highest political
theory of the Taipings. Thirdly, to work for equality and to respect the
able. The idea of equality was derived from their religious conception.
The respect for able men was carried through by their recommendation and
examination system in recruiting able civil servants and reprimanding
those who were lazy and unenergetic. The ideology was not bad per se,
but when tried out by the poorly educated executives, it seemed right,
but was actually wrong.[24] This is a summary of the evaluation of a
political theorist.

Lo Erh-kang gives a high estimation of the new systems of the
celestial court which is worth quoting at length.

"The Heavenly Kingdom of Great Peace founded a new dynasty and had all systems newly formed. This was not because the Heavenly King purposely made things new and strange, but for carrying through his revolutionary principles, because the Taiping revolution was not like the political revolution of Han Kao-tsu who overthrew the Ch'in, nor like the racial revolution of Ming T'ai-tsu who upset the Yüan. He (Hung) put down the worship of idols and decided that God was the most supreme; that was a religious revolution. He suppressed adultery, opium-smoking, drinking, gambling and other practices of cheating and coercion; that was a revolution of daily life. He got rid of the ownership of private property, making the treasuries and wealth the public possession; that was an economic revolution. He caused the old to have a proper place for their declining years, the strong to have places to make use of their abilities, the young to have means to grow up, the pitiful, widows, orphans, the solitary, the disabled and the ill to have funds to take care of them; that was a social revolution. He promoted popular literature and forbade the use of classical literary allusions; that was a cultural revolution. When we take a panoramic view of the revolution of the Taipings, it included political, racial, religious, the way of life, economic, social and cultural facets. He actually intended to turn the whole universe, to have the entire old world radically changed and to create a new world. In view of the vast scope and the far-reaching ideology, there is no match in the long past history....

Among some ten kinds of new systems, the religious, military and the land systems of the Celestial Court were the most important. The religion of the Heavenly Kingdom of Great Peace had a close concern with the spirit for establishing the state. It was derived from Christianity but the idea of the Heavenly Kingdom of Jesus Christ was particularly developed so as to widely spread the Gospel of equality and universal love among mankind. The ten heavenly commandments, which were decided, strictly forbade various evils of mankind and could renew the minds of people by means of religion. Even though the so-called ascents to heaven by the Heavenly King and the stories of a Heavenly Father and Heavenly Brother who descended and gave orders (through the mouths of the leaders) were criticized by the Christian missionaries, the Taiping religion naturally had its everlasting spirit. The purpose of the land system of the Celestial Dynasty was to make all people alike have land to plant, have food to eat, have clothes to wear, have money to use, have no places where distribution is uneven, and have no one who is not satiated and warm. Even though it was not put into practice, it was nevertheless an economic system worth our notice. Their military system was patterned after the Chou-li, having soldiers living among farmers so as to make soldiers and farmers alike. The practice was effective and it was also a valuable system.

Apart from this the local official system was an effective means to carry out the self-government of the people. The system of women-officials, and the examinations for women set up a precedent for woman-suffrage, while the Celestial calendar, which abruptly discarded the lunar calendar and used the solar calendar alone and which was enforced into actual use, preceded the change and the use of the solar calendar in the republican period. In literature, the promotion of popular writing, the advocacy of the abolition of frivolous expression and the use of effective words, the discard of the classical idioms and the esteem of expression of one's heart may also be said to be the forerunner of the new literature movement of the 4th of May (1919). All this is praiseworthy. The only points which may be criticized are their criminal law, which still followed the use of cruel punishment, of burning the head like a heavenly lamp and have the body dismembered by five horses, and in the system of rites where the color of emperors and officials of the monarchical period were still kept, and in the official system of the later period when the bestowal of feudal titles and reward was too excessive and lost the purpose of establishing officials and dividing ranks and incurred ridicule as being as worthless as rotten sheep's-heads. All these are unavoidable black spots of the Taiping systems. Nevertheless, the good and the bad points are not to be mutually beclouded. When we take a general review of the various new systems of the Celestial court, the greatness of the Heavenly King's revolution can be seen, and the false charge that he who is successful is the king while he who fails is a bandit is self-explanatory without waiting for argument."[25]

This is certainly a very sympathetic interpretation and full-mouthed praise of the Taiping reform. Although on the whole it is true, obviously there is exaggeration. The so-called social revolution such as the old, the young, and the solitary having means to be taken care of perhaps can hardly be substantiated. The corruption of the Heavenly King after taking Nanking and of all other officials and soldiers in later years should be mentioned. The sweeping statement that the scope of revolution and the far-reaching ideology are considered matchless in past history is also open to question.

In concluding this section, we may say that Hung, Feng, and Yang had great ingenuity and amazing creative powers. With a little knowledge of Christianity they could make their own story and create their own religion. With a limited education, they could create a new calendar, and a new political and social system to replace the old which had been in use with little challenge for more than two thousand years since the time of the Ch'in Dynasty.

The new light on the history of the Taiping Rebellion has thus been very briefly summed up in the preceding pages based on the publications available. It is not necessary to recapitulate what has already been mentioned about the far-reaching Taiping influence on political, social and other facets of modern China. Nor do we presume to claim that we have done justice in presenting the research work of all authors in the way that they may like us to do. On the whole, the new light on the history is still dim, limited, and fragmentary. Some controversies on small problems, even though they are in the modern period, may not be satisfactorily solved for a number of years to come, or forever. Many large issues still require a great deal of work. This short, critical digest of the materials about Taiping T'ien-kuo does not give much elaborate interpretation which would take much more space. It merely serves as an introductory essay for the reference of students of modern Chinese history, or as a little appetizer for a larger volume or volumes to be written by scholars.

NOTES

I. HISTORY OF THE STUDY OF THE TAIPING REBELLION

1. The Taiping rebellion has been variously dated as 1850-1864, 1851-1865, 1851-1866, and so on, but the appropriate one is 1851-1864. 1851 marks the first year of the Taiping kingdom which was overthrown in 1864, though the remnants of the movement were not entirely wiped out until as late as 1866. In this article the simpler form Taiping (rather than T'ai-p'ing) is frequently used.

2. See S. Y. Teng, "Chinese Historiography in the Last Fifty Years," The Far Eastern Quarterly, vol. VIII, no. 2 (February 1949), pp. 131-156.

3. Modern Chinese scholars consider the movement a revolution, not a rebellion. This idea is correct. In this essay, however, the idiomatic term, the Taiping rebellion, is still used for the convenience of quotations and for following English usage, but at the same time when new interpretations are introduced, the Taiping Revolution is employed.

4. The author's biography and the prefaces of the Hung Hsiu-ch'üan yen-i is reproduced in The Ta-feng 大風 no. 6 (1938), pp. 178-180. The criticism of this book is in the same magazine no. 23, pp. 735-6; and Chien Yu-wen considers this novel unreliable. (Ta-feng, no. 30, 939). The author, however, is quite a stylist.

5. According to the preface the book is based on the manuscript Hung-Yang chi-shih (洪楊紀事) which is actually the same work as Hung Yang lei-tsuan shih-lüeh (洪楊 類纂事畧). Both, however, are copied with modifications from the Tsei-ch'ing hui-tsuan (賊情彙纂), which will be mentioned momentarily in the text.

6. Such as Naitō Torajirō's 内藤虎次郎 "Some Historical Materials in the British Museum Relating to Taiping T'ien-kuo" (大英博物院所藏太平天國史料). Shirin 史林 vol. 10, no. 3 (October 1925), pp. 74-79. Naitō's article is based on the report of two Japanese scholars, Tanaka Suiichirō 田中萃一郎 , and Inaba Iwakichi 稲葉岩吉 .

7. Namely: T'ien-fu hsia-fan chao-shu, 天父下凡詔書 (1 and 2)

T'ien-ming chao-chih shu, 天命詔旨書

Pan-hsing chao-shu, 頒行詔書

T'ien-ch'ao t'ien-mou chih-tu, 天朝田畝制度

Chien T'ien-ching yu Chin-ling lun, 建天京於金陵論

Pien yao-hsüeh wei tsui-li lun, 駁妖穴為罪隸論

Yüan-tao chiu-shih ko, 原道救世歌 (should be
   T'ai-p'ing chiu-shih ko 太平救世歌)

Yüan-tao hsing-shih hsün, 原道醒世訓

Yüan-tao chüeh-shih hsün, 原道覺世訓

The last three are also found under the general title T'ai-p'ing chao-shu
太平詔書 which was written by Hung Hsiu-ch'üan in 1845 and 1846
representing his early religious thought. (See Rev. Theodore Hamberg,
The Visions of Hung-Siu-Tshuen, and Origin of the Kwang-Si Insurrection,
Reprinted, Peiping, 1935, p. 29).

8. Fourteen of the 16 documents are copied from the British Museum.

They are: T'ai-p'ing t'iao-kuei, 太平條規

Hsing-ying kuei-chü, 行營規矩

Chih-chun pan-hsing chao-shu tsung-mu, 旨准頒行詔書總目

Title page, name and official title of the Taiping calendar
   of 1861

Ch'ing-pan hsin-li tsou, 請頒新曆奏

T'ien-wang chao-chih, 天王詔旨 (1 and 2)

The Almanac, January 1861

The Almanac, January 1860

A Letter of Prince Chung to Prince Hu, 忠王致護王書

A Folk Song, 俚歌 , (Original note, taken from the
   T'ien-ch'ing tao-li shu)

A Dispatch of Prince of the First Order Ho-she to
   Gordon, 和碩親王致戈登書

A Letter of Chang Yü-ch'un to Gordon, 張遇春致戈登書

A Rubbing of the Character fu by Prince Kan, 干王福字碑

A Seal of Prince Kan, 干王印

9. Published by the Commercial Press for the National Compilation
Bureau. The contents may be given as below:

  (1) T'ien-fu Shang-ti yen-ti huang-chao, 天父上帝言題皇詔
  (2) Chiu-i-chao sheng-shu, 舊遺詔聖書
  (3) Hsin-i-chao sheng-shu, 新遺詔聖書
        A few pages used as an example from each of the first
        parts of the Old and New Testaments
  (4) T'ien-t'iao shu, 天條書
  (5) T'ai-p'ing chao-shu, 太平詔書
  (6) T'ai-p'ing li-chih, 太平禮制
  (7) T'ai-p'ing chün-mu, 太平軍目
  (8) T'ai-p'ing t'iao-kuei, 太平條規
  (9) T'ai-p'ing T'ien-kuo kuei-hao san-nien hsin-li, 太平天國
        癸好三年新曆
  (10) T'ai-p'ing hsin-yu shih-i-nien hsin-li, 太平辛酉十一年新曆
  (11) Yu-hsüeh shih, 幼學詩
  (12) T'ai-p'ing chiu-shih ko, 太平救世歌
  (13) Chao-shu kai-hsi pan-hsing lun, 詔書蓋璽頒行論
  (14) T'ien-ch'ao t'ien-mou chih-tu, 天朝田畝制度
  (15) T'ien-ch'ing tao-li shu, 天情道理書
  (16) Yü-chih ch'ien-tzu chao, 御製千字詔
  (17) Hsing-chün tsung-yao, 行軍總要
  (18) T'ien-fu shih, 天父詩
  (19) Hsing-shih wen, 醒世文
  (20) Wang chang- tz'u-hsiung ch'in-mu ch'in-erh kung-cheng
        fu-yin shu, 王長次兄親目親耳共證福音書
  (21) Ch'in-ting shih-chieh t'iao-li, 欽定士階條例
  (22) Yu-chu chao-shu, 幼主詔書
  (23) Ch'in-ting ying-chieh kuei-chen, 欽定英傑歸真
        or Ying-chieh kuei-chen

The first twenty titles were included in the official list of twenty-nine
Taiping publications (1860), but the last three were not mentioned in the
list because they were later publications.

10.　T'ai-p'ing T'ien-kuo kuan-shu pu-pien, 太平天國官書補編 was planned to include ten titles:

T'ien-li yao-lun, 天理要論

T'ai-p'ing T'ien-kuo chia-yin ssu-nien hsin-li, 太平天國甲寅四年新曆

Wu-wu pa-nien hsin-li, 戊午八年新曆

T'ai-p'ing li-chih, 太平禮制

Chi-wei chiu-nien hui-shih t'i, 己未九年會試題

Tzu-cheng hsin-pien, 資政新編

Kan-wang hung-pao chih, 干王洪寶製

Ch'in-ting chün-t'zu shih-lu, 欽定軍次實錄

Chu-yao hsi-wen, 誅妖檄文

T'ai-p'ing t'ien-jih, 太平天日

Some of these works have been published separately. See also Wang Chung-min's preface on the newly copied material, T'ai-p'ing T'ien-kuo kuan-shu pu-pien in the Kuo-li Pei-p'ing t'u-shu kuan kuan-k'an 國立北平圖書館館刊, vol. X, no. 6 (1936), pp. 25-29.

11.　Such as the T'ai-p'ing t'ien-jih published in I-ching, nos. 13, 14, 16; the Tzu-cheng hsin-pien in the same magazine, nos. 17, 18, 19; the Ch'in-ting chün-t'zu shih-lu in nos. 27, 28, 30, 31; and the Ying-chieh kuei-chen, 英傑歸真, in Jen-wen magazine vol. 6, no. 4, pp. 1-10; 6.5, pp. 11-20; 6.8, pp. 21-30; 6.9, pp. 31-36. The last work is also photolithographically reproduced in Hsiao I-shan's series. Other primary sources like the Yüeh-fei ch'i-shou ken-yu, 粵匪起手根由, Hung Hsiu-ch'üan lai-li, 洪秀全來歷, Hung Jen-kan tzu-shu, 洪仁玕自述, T'ai-p'ing ping-t'se, 太平兵冊, have all been published in Ching-shih, 經世 magazine. As for contemporary neutral or government sources in rare editions or manuscripts such as Fa-ni ch'u-chi, 髮逆初紀, Yüeh-fei chi-lüeh, 粵匪紀畧, Man-fen hui-pien 蠻氛匯編, Chiang-nan ch'un-meng-an pi-chi, 江南春夢菴筆記, and so on, they also have been discovered and used by scholars.

12.　According to Lo Erh-kang's study of the unlocated or missing Taiping works compiled by the Taipings,"T'ai-p'ing i-shu k'ao, 太平逸書考", in Hsien-tai hsüeh-pao, 現代學報, vol. I, nos. 2-3 (March 1947), pp. 43-48, there are six items:

> Ch'in-ting chih-tu tse-li chi-pien, 欽定制度則例集編
> San-kuo shih, 三國史
> Lü-wen, 律文, 177 articles
> Ch'in-ting ssu-shu wu-ching, 欽定四書五經
> T'ai-p'ing kuan-hsiu shih, 太平官修史
> Chung-wang hui-i chi-lüeh, 忠王會議輯畧

The first is perhaps the most important of all, and through the cooperation of bibliophiles throughout the world, it is hoped that some of the works mentioned above may turn up. As for the T'ien-li yao-lun 天理要論 which Hsiao I-shan considers unavailable in any library of the leading countries, Wang Chung-min believes it is a book based on Medhurst's T'ien-li yao-lun, 天理要論, which is in the Cambridge University Library. (Kuo-wen chou-pao, 國聞週報, vol. 13, no. 12 (March 1936), pp. 29-30).

II.   A GENERAL REVIEW OF THE WORKS OF THE TAIPING HISTORIANS

1.   See T'ai-p'ing chün Kuang-hsi shou-i-shih, cited hereafter as Shou-i-shih, pp. 37-40, for Chien's biographical information.

2.   The picture first appears in the front of the History of the Insurrection in China by M. M. Callery and Yvan, with the inscription "T'ien Te 天德 chief of the Insurrection." The same picture was adopted by Inaba Iwakichi, 稻葉岩吉, for his Complete History of the Ch'ing Dynasty (Ch'ing-ch'ao ch'üan-shih, 清朝全史) in which he deleted the two characters "T'ien Te" and replaced them with Hung Hsiu-ch'üan. Thereafter Chinese writers carelessly mistook T'ien Te or Hung Ta-ch'üan's picture as Hung Hsiu-ch'üan's and the error was not discovered until 1934 by Yü Ta-kang, 俞大綱, in Kuo-li Pei-p'ing t'u-shu-kuan kuan-k'an (vol. 8, no. 4, p. 28). The result is utilized here by Hsieh with the source indicated (Collection I, p. 5b).

3.   The book is also entitled Chin-ling kuei-chia chih-t'an, 金陵癸甲摭談, collected in the Man-fen hui-pien.

4. It was published by the Sheng-li ch'u-pan she, 勝利出版社, Chungking, 1944.

5. By the same publisher in 1941.

6. In the second entry of part I, pp. 17-30.

7. One is T'ai-p'ing T'ien-kuo chin-shih lu, 金石錄, which is a collection of Taiping metal and stone inscriptions including their seals, coins, poems, calligraphy, cannon, inscriptions, epitaphs, and so on. The other is T'ai-p'ing T'ien-kuo Kuang-hsi shou-i chih, 廣西首義志. (An Account of the Beginning of the Taiping revolution in Kwangsi). The material in the latter work is pretty much the same as the early part of Hung Hsiu-ch'üan's nien-p'u or chronological biography.

8. Such as T'ai-p'ing T'ien-kuo shih pien-wei chi, 史辨偽集, in which the problem of Hung Ta-ch'üan has been restudied and many other problems have been discussed; and the T'ien-ch'ao t'ien-mou chih-tu k'ao, 天朝田畝制度考 (The Land System of the Celestial Court). Both manuscripts have been turned over to the Commercial Press. In the winter of 1948 the author gave one more manuscript, T'ai-p'ing T'ien-kuo shih to Cheng-chung shu-chü for publication. This seems to be an overall history of the Taipings, but the author is not very satisfied with the old style of Chinese dynastic history in which the manuscript is written, and is trying to write a comprehensive history of this period following Western style.

9. Lo Erh-kang's Shih-men ju-chiao chi, 師門辱教記, Kuei-lin, 1944. This is a booklet in which Lo gives an account of his work under Hu Shih as the latter's assistant, and the training he received from his superior.

10. Ibid., p. 59.

11. The two volumes have been reviewed by the writer in Tientsin, Kuo-min jih-pao, May 2, 1947, p. 7, where comments and criticisms are given in more detail.

12. Ten chüan, three ts'e, published in 1944 and 1948 (revised edition) by Peiping, Ching-shih jih-pao she, 經世日報社. Some good articles

in the Fei-yü-kuan wen-ts'un deserve our attention. One is the article
in which Shih Ta-k'ai's letter to T'ang Yu-keng 唐友耕 is proved
spurious (chüan 4, pp. 109-188) and considerable material about Shih Ta-k'ai
is collected. The "Study on Hung Ta-ch'üan" (chüan 4, pp. 119-133) of which
only part A is published but which is to be continued, takes the side of the
existence of the man against the fabrication theory, and confirms the relation
of the early Taipings with the members of the Heaven and Earth society. The
section on the Taiping source material (chüan 4, pp. 153-155) is also noteworthy. A great deal of information about Li Hsiu-ch'eng (chüan 8, pp. 1-35)
and about the Taiping relations with secret societies (chüan 7, pp. 20-24,
27-41) is useful for reference. Two important documents, Hung Hsiu-ch'üan
lai-li 洪秀全來歷, and T'ai-p'ing T'ien-kuo kan-wang Hung Jen-kan
tzu-shu ping k'ao 太平天國干王洪仁玕自述並考,
are reproduced in the last volume (chüan 10, pp. 8-30), and many prefaces and
postfaces are reprinted in this work.

13. Fan Wen-lan (1891-   ), a native of Shaohsing, Chekiang, was a
graduate of National Peking University. He taught Chinese in Nankai
University and Peking University, and became dean of the College of
Literature and Science for Women of Peiping University. He compiled the
Cheng-shih k'ao-lüeh, 正史考署 (1932), Ch'ün-ching kai-lun, 羣經概論
(1933) and Chung-kuo t'ung-shih chien-pien, 中國通史簡編 (1947, in
cooperation with others). Cf. Hashikawa Tokio (compiler), Chūgoku bunka kai
jimbutsu sōkan 橋川時雄, 中國文化界人物總鑑, p. 294-95.

14. Such as Kakogawa Shōkan, Shinkoku sō-ran wa, 加古川將監, 清國
騷亂話 (1853); Yoshida Shōin, Shinkoku Kanhō ran ki, 吉田松陰, 清
國咸豐亂記 (1855) and so on. For informal contemporary writings, we
may mention Seiei Shujen, Shinzoku i-bun, 青衛主人, 清賊異聞 (1855);
Hanjōken Shujen, Gaihō Taihei ki, 磐上軒主人, 外邦太平記 (1854). At
that time Japanese scholars did not pay serious attention to the Chinese civil
war, so the value of these contemporary accounts is limited, and the accuracy
is not without question. The Shanghai Diary of 1862 (文久二年上海日記)
including three works written by Japanese diplomatic officers in Shanghai has
casual reference to Taiping but has little historical value.

15. The list is worked out by Yen Ch'eng-hui, 閻承惠 with the substantial help of the Japanese scholar, Masui Tsuneo, 增井經夫, who is a famous Taiping historian.

16. For Japanese magazine articles, attention may be paid to: Tanaka Tadao, Taihei Tengoku kakumei no shin kenkyū, 田中忠夫, 太平天國革命の新研究, in Tōa, 東亞 (vol. 5, no. 10, 1932); Akinaga Hajime, Taihei Tengoku gaikō shiron, 秋永肇, 太平天國外交史論 in Taihoku Teidai bunseigakubu seijigakuka nempō, 臺北帝大文政學部政治學科年報, vol. 7, section on international law; Suzue Genichi, Taihei Tengoku to gaikoku kankei, 鈴江言一, 太平天國と外國關係, Dairen, Mantetsu chōsa geppō, 滿鐵調查月報, vol. 14, no. 10 (1933); Masui Tsuneo (q.v.), Taihei Tengoku jidai, 太平天國時代, in Tokyo, Shin Chūgoku 新中國 no. 17 (1947); Fujiwara Sadamu, Taihei Tengoku undō, 藤原定, 太平天國運動, in Mantetsu chōsa geppō, vol. 19 no. 7 (1939), and so on.

17. S. Williams, Middle Kingdom, p. 624.

18. John Malcolm Bullock, Bibliography of the Gordons, Aberdeen, 1924, in which the works of and concerning Charles George ("Chinese") Gordon are listed in pp. 129-175. See also H. Cordier, Bibliotheca Sinica (1904), vol. 1, pp. 650-51.

19. See Eugene Boardman's review of this book in the Far Eastern Quarterly, vol. VIII, no. 1, (November 1948) pp. 108-109.

20. Vol. XVI (1932), pp. 544-614.

21. There is also a thesis by Shen Lien-chih under the title "Role du General Charles-George Gordon dans la repression de l'Insurrection des Thai Phing (Mars 1863-Juin 1864), Lyon, 1933. The thesis uses English and French sources almost entirely, except for a few Chinese works.

22. The sub-title is Ein Kapitel der menschlichen Tragikomodie; Nebst einem Uberblick uber Geschichte und Entwickelung Chinas. Halle, 1900, iv + 162 pages.

23. There is another work, Tai Ping Tien Guo, Rebellen unterm Kreuz by Lucy Cornelssen, published in Berlin, 1933, written as a novel based on a few secondary sources.

24. In the Bibliografiia Vostoka, or Bibliography of the Orient, nos. 5-6 (Leningrad, 1934), pp. 51-55, there is a list of Chinese sources on the Taiping movement. In no. 7 (1934), pp. 79-86, there is a bibliography of English, French, and German works about the Taiping but nothing in Russian is listed. See also Lawrence Krader, "Soviet Oriental Studies 1940-48," Far Eastern Survey, Vol. 17, no. 14 (July 1948), pp. 164-168; Rudolf Loewenthal, "Works on the Far East and Central Asia Published in the U.S.S.R., 1937-1947," The Far Eastern Quarterly, Vol. VIII, no. 2, (February 1949), pp. 172-183.

III. NEW LIGHT ON A FEW KNOTTY PROBLEMS

1. Mackie, Life of Tai-Ping-Wang, pp. 169, 278-79, and Brine, The Taiping Rebellion in China, pp. 124, 202, had T'ien-wang and Tai-Ping-Wang confused as one. Arthur Evans Moule, Half a Century in China (London, 1911), also writing from recollection says, "Some from a confusion of dialectic pronunciation erroneously gave it [Hung] King of Heavenly Virtue" (p. 29).

2. Charles MacFarlane, The Chinese Revolution (London, 1853) doubted the existence of Hung Ta-ch'üan, "We may safely say that there is not one word of truth in it" (pp. 88-89). Callery and Yvan mention, "The confession of Tien-te had produced a great sensation, and the particulars of his execution at Pekin were discussed, when all of a sudden it was ascertained that the dead Tien-te was apocryphal, and the real Tien-te was safe and sound...." (p. 139). This shows the early existence of the enigma. Other sources also cast doubt. Mackie, Life of Tai-Ping-Wang, pp. 194-196; Thomas T. Meadows says in The Chinese and their Rebellions "I am fully convinced that no such title, and consequently no person bearing such title, ever had existence among the Taepings themselves." (p. 241, footnote). Captain Fishbourne, Impression of China and the Present Revolution

(London, 1855), concludes, "I believe the story to have been one invented for the deception of the court, and that an ignorant insurgent was the man captured." (p. 77). Brine in Taiping Rebellion in China (London, 1862), pp. 137-38 took a more cautious attitude, though he expresses his doubts. Hung's confession is quoted in full by Yvan and Brine from Official Gazette or Ti-ch'ao in which Chinese documents were usually published.

3. Wen-tsung Hsien-huang-ti shih-lu, 文宗顯皇帝實錄, ch. 57, p. 21.

4. Chin-shih Chung-kuo mi-shih 近世中國秘史 by Mo-shih t'an-hu-k'o 捫蝨談虎客 vol. II, p. 105. According to Kuo T'ing-i, this pen name was Han K'ung-an 韓孔厂 which "someone thought to be Liang Ch'i-ch'ao." T'ai-p'ing T'ien-kuo shih-shih jih-chih, vol. I, p. 156

5. Chung-kuo li-shih yen-chiu-fa 中國歷史研究法 ch. 5, pp. 145-46. (Shanghai, 1933).

6. The review is reproduced in the Kuo-li Pei-p'ing t'u-shu-kuan kuan-k'an, vol. VIII No 4, pp. 5-9.

7. Ibid., pp. 21-29, in which the written confession in Chinese is for the first time printed from the Palace Museum archives and is reproduced in many other works.

8. The article of more than 20,000 words, first published in She-hui k'o-hsüeh (Tsing-hua University), vol. I, No. 3 (April 1936), pp. 679-724, in his T'ai-p'ing T'ien-kuo-shih ts'ung-k'ao, 18-62. Lo says, "This is an article written with the exhaustion of his energy and mind."

9. Hsieh's discussion of Hung Ta-ch'üan appears in his T'ai-p'ing T'ien-kuo shih-shih lun-ts'ung, pp. 125-136, and T'ai-p'ing T'ien-kuo ts'ung-shu shih-san chung, ts'e I, 3-6.

10. Fei-yü-kuan wen-ts'un, ch. 4, pp. 119-133 and ch. 7, pp. 29-41. Many of Hsiao's arguments are virtually taken from Yü Ta-kang's essay.

11. Chu's article, "The Enigma of T'ien-te Wang," Hsien-tai shih-hsüeh, Vol. 5, No. 1, is quoted in Chien's work.

12. Tseng Kuo-fan and the Taiping Rebellion, pp. 61-63.

13. T'ai-p'ing T'ien-kuo li-fa k'ao-ting, p. 33. Hung Ta-ch'üan was a new name of the opportunist after he joined the Taipings.

14. T'ai-p'ing T'ien-kuo shih-shih jih-chih, vol. I, pp. 153-175, especially pp. 166-168.

15. Chiao Liang 焦亮 or 焦大 was an educated man who also failed in government examination. He was then a monk for some time, and returned again to mundane life and became a leader of the Heaven and Earth Society in Hunan. The name of his wife was Hsü Yüeh-ying 許月英 and that of his brother was Chiao yü-ching 焦玉晶. They really had a few thousand strong causing trouble as bandits in southern Hunan. When the Taipings started a revolution at Chin-t'ien, Hung Ta-ch'üan went from afar to join them. Because of his potential power in Hunan, he was welcomed as an honorable guest and addressed as "Hsien-sheng" 先生, a teacher or scholar. (Note Chien does not agree with Lo's interpretation that this term was used by the Taipings to address captured scholars. Hsiao takes it as a chief or incense-burner of the secret society of Heaven and Earth). Later on in practical work Hung Ta-ch'üan and the God-worshippers were so different in opinions that the Taipings locked him with chains and left him behind. So he was arrested by the Manchu commander-in-chief, Sai-shang-a. The latter changed or inserted some words into Hung's confession in order to exaggerate his merit. His wife and younger brother adopted independent action to harass the government force, and finally, in 1856, the two chiefs surrendered to the governor of Hunan and they were executed by the local authority. (Lo Wen-chung kung tsou-kao 駱文忠公奏稿 ch. 4, p. 34).

16. Chien, Shou-i shih, pp. 270-284.

17. According to the Ch'ing shih-lu (Wen-tsung), on February 7, 1852 Sai-shang-a reported a victory for which Hsiang Jung and others were rewarded. (Ch. 50, pp. 7-8.) On March 1, Sai reported another small

victory (ch. 51, p. 11) and March 20 the emperor was greatly pleased
by the gradual approach of the government force to Yungan. (Ch. 52,
pp. 20b-23). Later on (April 7 and 17) more victories were memorialized
(ch. 54, pp. 4b, 17b-20b) and finally on April 28 Yungan was reported to
have been taken on April 6 and a rebel head Hung Ta-ch'üan arrested.
(ch. 55, pp. 24b-27b). The victorious military development shows that
there was no necessity to cause Sai-shang-a to fabricate Hung Ta-ch'üan
as an excuse for his failure and for securing a reward. Unexpectedly,
on April 29 an imperial decree reprimanded Sai and others for their
improper commanding, so as to cause the death of some officers (ch. 56,
p. 1b). Only Chin Yü-kuei 金玉貴, a second captain, was rewarded
with the military distinction of being called Pa-t'u-lu 巴圖魯
meaning "brave" in Manchu for his capture of Hung Ta-ch'üan. When the
Taipings attacked Kuei-lin, capital of Kwangsi after their flight from
Yungan, the court was amazed, and for this failure, Sai was degraded
four ranks and other high generals in the front were all punished.
(ch. 56, p. 22b).

18. The original document of the whole case and a detailed Peking
confession made before the joint examination board is still not
discovered.

19. "T'ai-p'ing T'ien-kuo and the T'ien-ti-hui," Shen-pao Monthly,
vol. 4, no. 1 (January 1935), p. 169.

20. T'ai-p'ing T'ien-kuo shih-shih jih-chih, vol. I, pp. 112-114.

21. The Visions of Hung-Siu-Tshuen and the Origins of the Kwang-si
Insurrection (reprinted by Yenching University, 1935), p. 56.

22. "A Study of the Relationship between the T'ai-p'ing T'ien-kuo
and the T'ien-ti-hui" in his T'ai-p'ing T'ien-kuo shih k'ao-cheng chi,
pp. 17-30.

23. Chien, Shou-i shih, pp. 211-219.

24. Brine, Taiping Rebellion in China, p. 113.

25. For example, see Hsiao I-shan's collected essays, Fei-yü-kuan....,
ch. 7, p. 7, and Shou-i shih, p. 218.

26. Tseng Kuo-fan says, "The numerousness of secret society members
in Hunan is well known by all men. When the Kwangsi bandits came to
Hunan more than a large half of the members of the Heaven and Earth
Society followed them." Tseng Wen-cheng kung tsou-kao, ch. 2, p. 2.

27. Kuo T'ing-i says that after 1849 the turmoils of Kwangtung and
Kwangsi came from the center of the Triad, which adopted T'ien-te as
the reign title or as the name of its emperor. That name was known
widely and was more popular than Hung Hsiu-ch'üan who may have made use
of the title, T'ien-te, because there were so many secret society members in the Taipings. T'ai-p'ing T'ien-kuo shih-shih jih-chih, vol. I,
p. 115. Note: According to T'ao Ch'eng-chang, Chiao-hui yüan-liu k'ao
陶成章，教會源流考 "On the Origin and the Development of
Secret Societies," p. 1, the San-ho-hui, San-tien-hui, the Triad, the
ko-lao-hui were all branches of the Heaven and Earth Society. Therefore, in this article these names are synonymous.

28. Half a Century in China, p. 31.

29. The story is mainly based on Hsieh Hsing-yao's study, a biography
of Ch'ien Chiang, T'ai-p'ing T'ien-kuo shih-shih lun-ts'ung, pp. 137-144
with his sources checked. There is another biography of Ch'ien Chiang in
Shih Pu-hua's Tse-ya-t'ang wen-chi 施補華，澤雅堂文集
(Block-print ed.,1893), ch. 5, pp. 17-18, which is not used by Hsieh. In
this source there is no mention of Ch'ien's part in agitating the local
people against the British. He irritated the awe-inspiring general,
I-ching 奕經 (d. 1853) by suggesting a strong policy against the British
and so he was put in jail, but was soon released. He voluntarily followed
Lin Tse-hsü in Lin's Sinkiang exile and served Lin reverently as a pupil
and contributed to irrigation in Ili. Thus the story is told differently.
In this text we adopt Ch'i Hsüeh-ch'iu, Chien-wen sui-pi 齊學裘，
見聞隨筆 (Block-print ed. 1868) ch. 6, p. 15.

30. Man-Ch'ing chi-shih 滿清紀事 , formerly a manuscript in the Imperial University Library, Tokyo, is now printed in Chin-shih Chung-kuo mi-shih, vol. II, pp. 91-92.

31. Lei's memorial is in the Palace Museum archives and reproduced in Hsieh's work.

32. T'ai-p'ing T'ien-kuo shih-shih jih-chih, vol. I, pp. 208-221, also cf. p. 264.

33. Fu I-ling, "Ch'ing-mo li-chin chih ch'i-yüan hsin-lun" 傅衣凌, 清末釐金之起源新論 , She-hui k'o-hsüeh 社會科學 vol. 2, No. 1-2 (June 1946), pp. 80-86.

34. The long letter is reproduced by photolithography in the T'ai-p'ing T'ien-kuo wen-shu in 1933 by the Palace Museum, Peiping. Page number is not indicated.

35. Hsieh's T'ai-p'ing T'ien-kuo shih-shih lun-ts'ung, pp. 186-211, points out much similarity between the thoughts expressed in the letter and Wang's other essays and correspondence. Lo's T'ai-p'ing T'ien-kuo ts'ung-kao, pp. 63-80, also reflects carefully Wang's writings. Kuo T'ing-i's Shih-shih jih-chih, vol. II, pp. 853-855, also considers the letter genuine.

36. Ch'en Chen-kuo, "Ch'ang-mao chuang-yüan Wang T'ao," 陳振國, 長毛狀元王韜 , I-ching, no. 33 (July 1937) pp. 41-45, presents some information from Wang's relatives. He lists other names which need not be mentioned one by one.

37. Ibid., pp. 41-42.

38. See two documents of the negotiations between the Peking court and the British and Chinese authorities in Shanghai, printed in Wen-hsien ts'ung-pien, no. 20 (October 1934), the 6th entry, page number is not indicated.

39. T'ao-yüan chih-tu 弢園尺牘 (Movable-type edition of 1880) ch. 5, pp. 12b-23. More proposals were made and printed in the same work, ch. 6, pp. 1-10. Many of Wang's suggestions, though minute are very

malignant, because he knew the inside story of both factions, and re-ported to the authorities of the two parties as a fifth columnist.

40. _Ibid._, ch. 8, p. 4b.

41. Ch'en Chen-kuo, p. 42.

42. _Ibid._, p. 42.

43. Io, p. 69.

44. Hsieh, p. 210.

45. He submitted three proposals in 1859 or 1860 discussing (1) methods of suppressing the Taipings, (2) methods of checking their advance, and (3) methods of bringing the rebels under control by consolidations or peaceful means. See T'ao-yüan wen-lu wai-pien, 弢園文錄外編 (Movable-type edition published by the author himself in 1880) ch. 7, pp. 3b-10b.

IV. THE NATURE, CAUSES, AND EARLY HISTORY OF THE REBELLION

1. P'eng Tse-i, T'ai-p'ing T'ien-kuo ko-ming ssu-ch'ao, ch. 1, especially p. 19, has the similar idea.

2. Preface to his T'ai-p'ing T'ien-kuo shih-shih lun-ts'ung, p. 1

3. Chin-t'ien chih-yu, p. 199.

4. Ch'ing-tai shih 清代史 (History of the Ch'ing Dynasty, the Commercial Press, 1944), p. 161.

5. Chung-kuo hsien-tai ko-ming yün-tung shih 中國現代革命運動史, compiled by a Committee on Modern Chinese History and published in 1938 by Chung-kuo ch'u-pan she 中國出版社 in Chung-king, p. 31.

6. Chu Ch'i-hua, Chung-kuo chin-tai she-hui shih chieh-p'ou 朱其華, 中國近代社會史解剖 (An Analysis of Modern Chinese Society, Shanghai, 1933), p. 104.

7. Hsieh Nung-shan, <u>Chung-kuo nung-min chan-cheng chih shih-ti yen-chiu</u> 薛農山，中國農民戰爭之史的研究(A Historical Survey of Chinese Peasants' War, Shanghai, Shen-chou kuo-kuang she, 1935), p. 287. The book has been translated into Japanese.

8. Chang Chien-fu, <u>Chung-kuo chin-pai-nien shih chiao-ch'eng</u>, 張建甫，中國近百年史教程 (A Syllabus of Chinese History of the Last Hundred Years, Hongkong, Wen-hua kung-ying she, 1947), p. 31.

9. <u>Chung-kuo chin-tai shih</u> 中國近代史 (Modern Chinese History, Shanghai, Kai-ming shu-chü, 1946), pp. 43-44.

10. <u>Shou-i shih</u>, p. 94.

11. Liu I-cheng, <u>Chung-kuo wen-hua shih</u> 柳詒徵，中國文化史 (History of Chinese Civilization, Nanking, Chung-shan shu-chü, 1932), vol. II, 404, and Chin Chao-feng, <u>Ch'ing-shih ta-kang</u> 金兆豐，清史大綱 (An Outline of the Ch'ing History, Shanghai, Kai-ming shu-chü, 1935), pp. 407-414.

12. Nashimoto Yūhei, <u>Taihei Tengoku kakumei</u>; Sano Gaku, <u>Taihei Tengoku kakumei</u>; Tanaka Tadao's new study of the Taiping revolution in <u>Tōa</u>, vol. V, no. 10 (October 1932), pp. 31-41; Nahara Shira's article in the <u>Sekai rekishi taikei</u>, vol. 9, pp. 151-158, and so forth, are all sympathetically written with emphasis on the agricultural background.

13. Hobson's report is quoted in Macfarlane, <u>The Chinese Revolution</u>, p. 127.

14. Hsiao Kung-ch'üan, <u>Chung-kuo cheng-chih ssu-hsiang shih</u>, 蕭公權，中國政治思想史 (History of Chinese Political Thought, Shanghai, the Commercial Press, 1946), pp. 307-08.

15. Hsiao-I-shan, <u>Ch'ing-tai t'ung-shih</u>, 蕭一山，清代通史 (Shanghai, the Commercial Press, 1927), I, pp. 400-402. See also <u>Tung-hua-lu</u>, (K'ang-hsi) 6, p. 4b.

16. Wang Hsiu-ch'u, <u>Yang-chou shih-jih chi</u>, 王秀楚，揚州十日記 , which has been translated by Lucien Mao as "A Memoir of the Ten Days' Massacre in Yangchow," <u>T'ien Hsia Monthly</u> Vol. 4, no. 5, (May 1937), pp. 515-537. It has also been translated into German and French.

17. Such as the three wholesale massacres in the district of Chia-ting, Kiangsu, 1645, and in various districts of Kwangtung as recorded in Huang Hung-shou, Ch'ing-shih chi-shih pen-mo 黃鴻壽 ，清史紀事本末 (Shanghai, Chung-hua shu-chü, 1915), ch. 10, pp. 3-6, and Chien Yu-wen, Shou-i-shih, pp. 90-91.

18. Ming-i tai-fang lu, 明夷待訪錄 , especially the chapters on Prince, on Minister and on Jurisprudence.

19. See his patriotic poems in his collected writings and his Jih-chih-lu, 日知錄 , and T'ien-hsia chün-kuo li-ping shu, 天下郡國利病書 。

20. See his Tu-t'ung-chien-lun, 讀通鑑論 , in which he expresses his nationalistic and progressive ideas here and there. He would rather have China governed by a usurper than to be dominated by a foreign people.

21. Sheng-tsu Jen-huang-ti sheng-hsün, 聖祖仁皇帝聖訓 ch. 8, p. 2.

22. It is not easy to trace the exact date of the beginning of selling official ranks in the Ch'ing dynasty. Lo Erh-kang gives it as 1649 (T'ai-p'ing T'ien-kuo shih-kang, p. 30), but there is no way to trace or verify the source. In Teng Ssu-yü's Chung-kuo k'ao-shih chih-tu shih 鄧嗣禹 ，中國考試制度史, (History of Chinese Examination System), he traced it to 1676 (Nanking, 1936), pp. 347-48. Ch'ing-shih kao, ch. 119, p. 1b, states that the selling of civil ranks began in 1674. Thus Lo Erh-kang made a mistake here.

23. "Ku Ts'ung, Ch'ing-fen fan-chien chung-ming-ch'i su, 顧琮 ，請分繁簡重名器疏 ," Ho Ch'ang-ling, Huang-ch'ao ching-shih wen-pien, 賀長齡 ，皇朝經世文編 , ch. 17, p. 17.

24. Cf. Lo Erh-kang, T'ai-p'ing T'ien-kuo shih-kang, p. 32.

25. Shih-liao hsün-k'an, 史料旬刊 , no. 14 (October 1930), pp. 490-498; Hsüeh Fu-ch'eng, Yung-an pi-chi 薛福成 ，庸盦筆記 , ch. 3, pp. 3b-7b; and Hummul, Eminent Chinese, pp. 288-290, in which there is a succinct biography of Ho-shen written by Knight Biggerstaff; Meng Shen, Ch'ing-shih chiang-i 孟森 ，清史講義 , (Shanghai, Wen-hua fu-wu she, 1947), pp. 390-410 has some good material about Ho-shen's bribery based on Korean Shih-lu.

26. Archives on Ho-shen's case in Jen-wen, Vol. VI, no. 6 (May 1935) p. 3.

27. Lung Ch'i-jui, Ching-te-t'ang wen-chi, 龍啟瑞，經德堂文集 , ch. 3, p. 23 in Yüeh-hsi wu-chia wen-ch'ao 粵西五家文鈔 (block-print edition of 1898).

28. T'ai-p'ing T'ien-kuo ch'ien-chi in his T'ai-p'ing T'ien-kuo ts'ung-shu shih-san-chung, ts'e, I, p. 4.

29. The leader of this uprising was Wang Lun, 王倫, and the general who suppressed it was Shu-ho-te, 舒赫德, and the documents relating to this episode were published in 1781 under the title, Chiao-pu Lin-ch'ing ni-fei chi-lüeh, 劉捕林清逆匪紀略 , 16 chüan.

30. See the biography of A-kuei, Ch'ing-shih kao, ch. 324, pp. 4b-5.

31. The biography of Ch'ai Ta-chi, 柴大紀, Ch'ing-shih lieh-chuan, 清史列傳, ch. 25, p. 41b.

32. The official documents concerning the suppression of the rebellion are collected in the Chiao-p'ing san-sheng hsieh-fei fang-lüeh, 劉平三省邪匪方畧 , published in or about 1810.

33. The official documents are collected under the title, Lin Ch'ing chiao-an, 林清教案 , in Ku-kung chou-k'an, nos. 195-236.

34. Ch'ing-shih kao, ch. 386, p. 2b.

35. Ching-shih wen-pien, ch. 58. Miao Tzu's 繆梓 memorial. Cf. Lo Erh-kang's outline history, p. 16.

36. Ch'ing-ch'ao wen-hsien t'ung-k'ao, 清朝文獻通考 (the Commercial Press edition, Shanghai, 1936), ch. 4, p. 4887. Note: 1 ch'ing = 100 mou = 15.13 acres. See Herbert A. Giles' A Chinese-English Dictionary under ch'ing.

37. Chao-lien, Hsiao-t'ing hsü-lu, 昭槤 , 嘯亭續錄, ch. 1, pp. 63-64, under the item, "Rich people of this dynasty" (Block-print edition of 1810).

38. Wang Ying, T'ai-p'ing T'ien-kuo ko-ming ch'ien-hsi ti t'u-ti wen-t'i 王瑛，太平天國革命前夕的土地問題，"The Land Problem on the Eve of the Taiping Revolution," Chung-shan wen-hua chiao-yü kuan chi-k'an, 中山文化教育館季刊, vol. III, no. 1 (1936). We regret we are unable to locate this issue but get a summary from P'eng Tse-i's work, pp. 12, and 25-26. However, the same author, Wang Ying, has a shorter article under a similar title in the Shih-huo 食貨 semi-monthly, vol. II, no. 3 (July 1935), pp. 39-44, in which he concludes that because of the fact that much land was occupied by Manchu banners, high interest was prevalent and the annexation of land by great landlords was common. The multitudes of farmers had a very poor life.

39. A special article is prepared by Fu I-ling under the title, T'ai-p'ing T'ien-kuo shih-tai ti ch'üan-kuo k'ang-liang ch'ao, 傳衣凌，太平天國時代的全國抗糧潮 ("The Tide of Refusing to pay Land-tax in the whole Country during the Time of the Taiping Rebellion," Ts'ai-cheng chih-shih, 財政知識, vol. III, no. 3 (September 1943), pp. 31-39.

40. Wang yü-ch'üan, Ch'ing-mo t'ien-fu yü nung-min, 王毓銓，清末田賦與農民, "The Land Tax in the Late Ch'ing and the Farmers", Shih-huo semi-monthly, vol. III, no. 5 (February 1936), pp. 43-54 in which he finds that an agrarian revolution is a natural outcome from the regular as well as numerous irregular and illegal charges. See Hsia Nai, T'ai-p'ing T'ien-kuo ch'ien-hou Ch'ang-chiang ko-sheng chih t'ien-fu wen-t'i, 夏鼐，太平天國前後長江各省之田賦問題，"The Land Tax of the Yangtze Provinces before and after the Taiping Rebellion," Tsing Hua Hsüeh-pao, 清華學報，vol. X, no. 2 (April 1935), pp. 409-474, especially pp. 410-428. In Hsia's good article he clearly presents the heavy taxation and the urgent necessity of a reduction of the tax. For the purpose of winning the hearts of the people in the war-torn Yangtze area, the tax was cut nominally by the government beginning from 1858, actually from 1855. See Yung Wing's opinion on this point in My Life in China and America, p. 118.

41. Kao-tsung Shun-huang-ti shih-lu, 高宗純皇帝實錄,
ch. 405, p. 19b. Wen-tsung Hsien-huang-ti shih-lu, 文宗顯皇
帝實錄, ch. 50, p. 33b.

42. It is to be noted that the statistical figure for the total
acre of cultivated land is not often given in the Ch'ing shih-lu. We
have to check this figure from other sources. It is the same in the
Ch'ing-ch'ao wen-hsien t'ung-k'ao, ch. 2, p. 4865.

43. This figure is not mentioned in the Shih-lu. It is quoted in
the Wen-hsien t'ung-k'ao, ch. 4, pp. 4890-91. Note: These figures
are also given in a good Japanese article on the various phenomena
of overpopulation near the end of Ch'ing and the Taiping T'ien-kuo
movement in the Mantetsu chōsa geppō, vol. 9, no. 7 (July 1939), pp. 1-71

44. Ch'ing-ch'ao wen-hsien t'ung-k'ao, ch. 3, p. 4871.

45. I, 210. A great deal of similar information appears in the
Trade and Administration of China by the same author.

46. Lo Wen-chung kung tsou-kao (undated), ch. 8, pp. 13-14. Cf.
Lo Erh-kang's outline history, p. 16.

47. T'ai-p'ing shan-j'en, [pseud., Hsieh Hsing-yao?], Tao-kuang-
ch'ao yin-huang wen-t'i, 太平山人，道光朝銀荒問題,
"The Problem of the Dearth of Silver in the Tao-kuang Period," Chung-ho
yüeh-k'an, 中和月刊 , Vol. I, no. 8 (August, 1940), pp. 61-75.

48. These figures have been checked. The first one appears in the
Ta-ch'ing hui-tien, 大清會典 (Chia-ch'ing period), ch. 11, p. 10b.
The other is in Hsiao I-shan's Ch'ing-tai t'ung-shih, "The middle volume"
or II, 340, where a list of the total arable land is given.

49. These figures in pages 67-68 of T'ai-p'ing shan-jen's article
are based on Wang Ch'ing-yün, Shih-ch'ü yü-chi, 王慶雲，石渠餘紀
ch. 3, pp. 2b-3.

50. "The Chronological and Seasonal Distribution of Floods and
Droughts in Chinese History, 206 B.C. - A.D. 1911," Harvard Journal

of Asiatic Studies, Vol. 6, nos. 3-4 (February 1942), pp. 273-311. See especially pp. 278-279, 281, and passim.

51. There are several studies on unusual catastrophes such as "Wang Shu-lin, Ch'ing-tai tsai-huang, i-ko t'ung-chi ti yen-chiu," 王樹林清代災荒，一個統計的研究, "A Statistical Study of Famines in the Ch'ing Dynasty," She-hui hsüeh-chieh, 社會學界, vol. IV (June 1932), pp. 123-227. The accuracy of this study seems to be dubious. T'ang Hsiang-lung, Tao-kuang mo-nien pei tsai hsien-shu piao, 湯象龍，道光末年被災縣數表, "A List of the Number of Districts Affected by Famine in the end of Tao-kuang period," in Chung-kuo chin-tai ching-chi-shih yen-chiu chi-k'an, 中國近代經濟史研究集刊, seems to be more accurate. P'eng Tse-i, op. cit., pp. 23-24, gives a list of famine in Kwangsi from 1821-1850. There are other studies on this subject which need not be mentioned one by one.

52. It is to be noted that reports and records of famine in Chinese sources are not very accurate or detailed. The accuracy of reports apparently depends upon the good service of a governor. If he is not dutiful, he ignores or disregards the distress of the people under his jurisdiction. For instance, the terrible condition of the Hunan famine of 1850 was vividly and frequently described by the author's grandparents in that province and yet there is little mention of it in the Ch'ing shih-lu.

53. Chien Yu-wen, Shou-i-shih, p. 173.

54. Ibid., pp. 173-176; Chang Hsiao-ming, T'ai-p'ing T'ien-kuo ko-ming shih, 張霄鳴，太平天國革命史 (Shen-chou kuo-kuang she, Shanghai, 1932), pp. 79-85, Hsieh Nung-shan, op. cit., pp. 264-286, 298-306.

55. Fan Wen-lan, T'ai-p'ing T'ien-kuo ko-ming yün-tung, p. 7.

56. Tseng Wen-cheng kung tsou-kao, ch. 1, pp. 36-40.

57. See Tseng's biography in the Eminent Chinese, pp. 751-756.

58. A memorial discussing the elimination of soldiers submitted to the emperor on April 10, 1851. Tseng Wen-cheng kung tsou-kao, ch. 1, p. 24.

59. Wu-lan-t'ai's memorial was translated into English from The Peking Gazette by Thomas Meadows and is quoted in his book, The Chinese and Their Rebellions, p. 160.

60. Hsieh-shan chü-shih [Hsia Hsieh] , Yüeh-fen chi-shih, 謝 山居士[夏燮], 粤氛紀事 , ch. 1, p. 1.

61. Works of Marx and Engels, Vol. VIII, pp. 210-211. In the North China Herald, no. 340, January 31, 1857, there is a short essay by "The Old Cathay" who says that "the main cause of the Insurrection was the war with Great Britain."

62. As a Cantonese, Chien Yu-wen explains the characteristics and the historical position of the people of Kwangtung very clearly in his Shou-i shih, pp. 89-92, 112.

63. "On the 23rd October, 1849, fifty-eight vessels of a pirate fleet were destroyed in a bay on the confines of China and Cochin China by a British naval force. But the crews escaped mostly on shore, carrying their arms with them.... We find from the Peking Gazette that a formidable body of rebels was waging open war with the forces of the local government in the southern borders of Kwang se." The Chinese and Their Rebellions, pp. 137-138.

64. Many Taiping leaders including Hung Hsiu-ch'üan and Yang Hsiu-ch'ing were mentioned by the Tsei-ch'ing hui-tsuan (ch. 1) as having worked as members to convey "foreign goods" (opium) when, according to Yung Wing, "The overland transport trade between Siang Tan [Hunan]and Canton was immense. It gave employment to at least one hundred thousand porters, carrying merchandise over the Nan Fung pass, between the two cities, and supported a large population along both sides of the thoroughfare. Steam, wars and treaties of very recent dates have broken up this system of labor." (pp. 87-88). In other words after the treaty of Nanking, these 10,000 odd porters were jobless. For instance Wu Ju-hsiao,

吳如孝 , an interpreter for foreign merchants in Canton, joined the Taipings and was later made Prince Ku. (Shou-i-shih, p. 159). This explains why jobless workers from Canton joined the Taipings.

65. The two references appear in Yung Wing, op. cit., pp. 122, 118, respectively.

66. P'eng Tse-i, p. 19.

67. Chien, Shou-i-shih, pp. 51-54, and Lo Erh-kang, Hung Hsiu-ch'üan, p. 1, and Lo, Chin-t'ien ch'i-i-ch'ien Hung Hsiu-ch'üan nien-p'u, p. 1.

68. Hung's name was reported as Chu, 朱 , Chiao, 焦 , , Cheng, 鄭 , and others. After the discovery of the genealogy of Hung's family and of the field investigations by Chien and others at Hung's birthplace, the various notions or imaginations of the real name of the Celestial King have definitely been attested without further doubt and Hsieh also expressed his consent. See Chien Yu-wen, Shou-i-shih, pp. 55-56, and Hsieh Hsing-yao, T'ai-p'ing T'ien-kuo shih-shih lun-ts'ung, pp. 118-136. Cf. also Lo Hsiang-lin, T'ai-p'ing T'ien-kuo T'ien-wang chia-shih k'ao-cheng, 羅香林 , 太平天國天王家世考證 , "A Critical Study of the Family History of the Celestial King of the Taiping T'ien-kuo," Kuang-chou hsüeh-pao, 廣州學報 vol. I, no. 2 (April 1937), pp. 1-20, which reveals little beyond Chien's research.

69. Kuo-yu was Hung Hsiu-ch'üan's grandfather. Chien, Shou-i-shih, p. 61.

70. I-ching, no. 2 (March 1936), pp. 3-5, and Theodore Hamberg, op. cit., pp. 1-2, and Shou-i-shih, pp. 61-63.

71. Lo Erh-kang, T'ai-p'ing T'ien-kuo shih ts'ung-k'ao, pp. 91-95, and the Hung Hsiu-ch'üan, pp. 3-4. Chien, Shou-i-shih, pp. 59-60; and Lo Hsiang-lin, K'o-chia yen-chiu tao-lun, 羅香林,客家研究導論 (An Introduction to the Study of Hakkas in its Ethnic, Historical, and Cultural Aspects, Canton, 1933), especially chapters 7 and 8.

72. Chien, Shou-i-shih, pp. 65-66, and Lo Erh-kang, Hung Hsiu-ch'üan, p. 4.

73. Only Chien Yu-wen has traced the history of Hung's teacher (Shou-i-shih, pp. 66-68), but his work on this point should be accepted with caution.

74. Ibid., p. 65.

75. Ibid., pp. 68-69. This coincides with our conception, that is, for curiosity's sake, Hung must have glanced over the pamphlets.

76. The sources assigned the date of Hung's receiving of the nine pamphlets in 1836 are Theodore Hamberg's writings, and Hung Hsiu-ch'üan lai-li in I-ching, no. 25, and Chien Yu-wen, Shou-i-shih, p. 68. Those putting the date in 1837, are the confession of Hung Jen-kan, and Lo Erh-kang's Chin-ling ch'i-i-ch'ien Hung Hsiu-ch'üan nien-p'u. When Hamberg recorded the date of 1836 he put a footnote saying, "It may also have been some time before that period." (p. 8). That indicates that he and his informant, Hung Jen-kan, were not so sure about the date. Thomas Meadows says it was "probably in 1833" (p. 75). The latter part was agreed by P'eng Tse-i in his T'ai-p'ing T'ien-kuo ko-ming ssu-ch'ao, (p. 6). I have some idea about this date, too, but it behooves me to express it elsewhere.

77. Hung Jen-kan's written confession in the I-ching, no. 20 (December 1936), p. 9.

78. In the earlier publications recording Hung's visions, he saw only an old man and a middle-aged man standing behind him. In later versions the old man was interpreted as God, and the middle-aged, Jesus Christ. Obviously the story was invented to help his religious politics.

79. Kuo-li Pei-p'ing t'u-shu-kuan kuan-k'an, vol. VIII, no. 4, p. 22.

80. (1). "Hung Hsiu-ch'üan lai-li" written in 1852, I-ching, no. 25 (March 1937), pp. 43-44. (2). Theodore Hamberg, The Visions of Hung-Sui-Tshuen, 1854. (3). Wang chang, tz'u-hsiung ch'in-mu, ch'in-erh kung-cheng fu-yin shu, written in 1860 in T'ai-p'ing T'ien-kuo ts'ung-shu, t'se 8. (4). Ying-chieh kuei-chen, written in 1861, T'ai-p'ing T'ien-kuo ts'ung-shu, t'se 10. (5). T'ai-p'ing t'ien-jih, written by Hung Hsiu-ch'üan in 1848, but not printed until 1862. I-ching, 13, 14, 16.

81. Ku Chieh-kang, Ku-shih pien, vol. I (Peking, 1926), p. 60.

82. P. 7.

83. Shou-i-shih, pp. 78-79.

84. Shou-i-shih, p. 86.

85. Ibid., pp. 86-89 and Lo Hsiang-lin, K'o-chia yen-chiu, pp. 245-247.

86. Cf. Meadows, op. cit., p. 89.

87. For example: T'ien-che hu t'ing, ch'ieh ti-che-hu fu erh. "天者乎聽，且地者乎附耳 " (1.16). Wu-lao-te k'o-huai-chih-liang, nai-i-te ts'un-yü ch'ang-sheng-chih-lao,"勿勞得可壞之糧，乃以得存於常生之勞" (4.1).

88. Wang Sheng-chün is given by Lo Erh-kang is his nien-p'u as Huang, 黃 . According to Chien Yu-wen, it should be Wang, because "wang" was a taboo and it was replaced in Taiping official publications by "Huang." See Chien, Chin-t'ien chih-yü, pp. 19-20.

89. Henri Cordier, Histoire des Relations de la Chine avec les Puissances occidentales, 1860-1900. Tome 1, p. 169n.

90. Shou-i-shih, pp. 129-130.

91. Ibid., pp. 104-112, 131-135, and passim; and Chin-t'ien chih-yu, pp. 20-27.

92. Chien Yu-wen considers this point as his new discovery, otherwise he cannot understand why Yang Hsiu-ch'ing, an illiterate, soon had a higher position than Feng. It is because Yang's elder sister was the mother of the rich man, Tseng Yü-chen, 曾玉珍 , who was a patron of Hung and an employer of Feng as a teacher. Because of Yang's elderly position in the Tseng family, both Hung and Feng had to respect him. See Chin-t'ien chih-yu, pp. 28-29.

93. Shou-i-shih, pp. 169-170; Lo, Hung Hsiu-ch'üan, pp. 28-30.

94. Chin-t'ien chih-yu, pp. 32-44.

95. See the biography of Shih Ta-k'ai by Lo Erh-kang in his Hung Hsiu-ch'üan, pp. 99-113. Chien's study of Shih Ta-k'ai's family history in his Chin-t'ien chih-yü, pp. 159-168. Hsieh Hsing-yao considers Shih Ta-k'ai a close partisan of Yang Hsiu-ch'ing (see T'ai-p'ing T'ien-kuo ts'ung-shu shih-san chung, t'se 1, pt. II, p. 19) and Tu Li-ho's 都履和 article on the arrest of Shih Ta-k'ai in Hsin Chung-hua, 新中華 , vol. III, no. 9 (September 1934), pp. 67-77 had also some new material.

96. See note 64.

97. Shou-i-shih, pp. 218-219 and Chin-t'ien chih-yü, pp. 51-52.

98. For instance, Li Hsiu-ch'eng kung-t'zu put it in the sixth moon; Hung Hsiu-ch'üan's biography in the Tsei-ch'ing hui-tsuan assigns it to the tenth moon, Meadows (p. 144) the beginning of October; Brine (p. 12), November or December and Kuo T'ing-i, Shih-shih jih-chih, I, 78, between September and November. The year is unanimously given as 1850.

99. Shou-i-shih, pp. 203-207. Lo Erh-kang at first believed in a different date, but later he gave up his original to accept Chien's conclusion, that it is January 1, 1851. See Lo's biography of Hung Hsiu-ch'üan, p. 33; and Hung Hsiu-ch'üan nien-p'u, p. 64.

V. NEW LIGHT ON THE MILITARY DEVELOPMENT

1. Cf. the biography of Hung Hsiu-ch'üan in the Eminent Chinese, I, 263.

2. Shou-i-shih, p. 208.

3. Ibid., pp. 302-303

4. Kara-Murza, Georgii S., Taipiny: velikoe krest'ianskoe i. Taipinskoe gosudarstvo v Kitae, 1850-1864, p. 61, in which there are a couple of sentences saying that the Russian scholar Skachkov lived (1853) in Peking. He asked a Chinese whether he thought the Taipings would come to Peking. The man replied "yes". Asked whether he feared them, he said "no". Fan Wen-lan's Tai-p'ing T'ien-kuo, p. 16, quotes

Asia and Russia by Marx and Engels as saying that the court gave the order, which cannot be found in the Ch'ing shih-lu.

5. Chien Yu-wen, "T'ai-p'ing T'ien-kuo pei-fa-chün chan-shih," 太平天國北伐軍戰史, "A War History of the North Expedition Force of the Taiping T'ien-kuo," Ta-feng 96 (August 22, 1941), p. 3241.

6. Hsieh, "T'ai-p'ing chün pei-fa shih", 太平軍北伐史, A History of the Taiping Northern Expedition, in the Tai-p'ing T'ien-kuo ts'ung-shu shih-san-chung, t'se 1, pp. 13-20. Chien's War History of the Taiping Northern Expedition Force in Ta-feng, no. 93 (July 5, 1941), pp. 3128-3133; 94 (July 22), 3168-3172; 95 (Aug. 5), 3205-3209; 96 (Aug. 22), 3238-3241; 97 (Sept. 5), 3278-3282; 98 (Sept. 22), 3315-3320; 99 (Oct. 5), 3351-3354. Hsieh's account is limited to the Honan section; Chien carries the enterprise from the beginning to the end.

7. Chien Yu-wen, A Review of the Rise and Fall of the Taiping T'ien-kuo, in his Chin-t'ien chih-yu, pp. 199-200.

8. Ch'i Chi-kuang, a native of Shantung, was a military genius who expelled Japanese invasions in the coast of Chekiang and Fukien, while it was well-nigh an impossible job for other generals. He is the author of Lien-ping shih-chi 練兵實紀, and Chi-hsiao hsin-shu, 紀效新書, both in military training, strategy, and so on. His method of militia organization was adopted by Tseng Kuo-fan and others in the Ch'ing dynasty. Cf. his biography in the Ming shih, ch. 212, pp. 11-18.

9. In Hsiao's T'ai-p'ing T'ien-kuo ts'ung-shu, t'se 2, 34 pages.

10. Stanley Lane-Poole, Life of Sir Henry Parkes (London, 1894), I, 432.

11. Cf. Li Hsiu-ch'eng kung-tz'u, ch. 1, p. 11, and Chien, Chin-t'ien chih-yu, p. 206.

12. A long description can be written about the government generals and soldiers with a bibliography of Chinese and Western sources. To mention a few, there were Hsiang Jung who put his son in lucrative positions in the army, Chou T'ien-chüeh who was nearly eighty years old and was still a field commander against the rebels, and Sai-shang-a who

was a civilian official ignorant of military affairs and provincial conditions. Government soldiers were corrupt, untrained, disordered, and so on. (Shou-i-shih, pp. 231-32). Wang T'ao also noticed, "The deterioration of today's military system is almost the same as that near the end of the Ming. Whenever they enter a town, the town will be empty, whenever they pass a village, a disturbance would be made. They look upon the people as dogs and sheep; they fear the bandits as tigers and wolves. Those above them gloss over things and rely on intrigues and briberies for advancement, making exaggerated reports of merits in order to secure a reward." T'ao-yüan wen-lu wai-pien, ch. 7, p. 3b. This is a first-hand account by a man who knows the conditions of the two sides.

13. Callery and Yvan, op. cit., p. 251.

14. Tsei-ch'ing hui-tsuan, ch. 8.

15. In the T'ai-p'ing T'ien-kuo ts'ung-shu, t'se 2.

16. Hua Kang, T'ai-p'ing T'ien-kuo fan-ch'ing chan-cheng ti chan-lüeh yen-chiu, 華崗，太平天國反清戰爭的戰畧研究， "A Study of the Strategy of the Taiping T'ien-kuo's war against the Manchu", Ch'ün-chung 羣衆, vol. VIII, no. 15 (Sept. 16, 1944), pp. 432-437 and Yang Sung, Lun T'ai-p'ing T'ien-kuo shih-wu-nien ko-ming chan-cheng ti ching-kuo chi-ch'i chan-lüeh-shang-ti t'so-wu, 楊松，論太平天國十五年革命戰爭的經過及其戰畧上的錯誤, "A Discussion of the fifteen year revolutionary war of the Taiping T'ien-kuo and its Strategic Errors" in the same magazine, vol. IV, no. 12 (May 10, 1940), pp. 365-370, 780. A large part of the essential points of these articles have been digested in the text. Fan Wen-lan's book on the Taiping also pays due attention to military tactics.

17. Lo Erh-kang, T'ai-p'ing T'ien-kuo ts'ung-k'ao, p. 191.

18. According to a manuscript copy of Hsiang Jung's memorials about the Taiping T'ien-kuo, in Tsing Hua University library, there is a paragraph saying, "A rumor, spread by the rebels, deceitfully

claims that the prayer they read can avoid bullets, and when a bullet comes, if a soldier's hand touches a small flag, then it will not hurt his body" - reproduced in Lo Erh-kang's T'ai-p'ing T'ien-kuo-shih ts'ung-k'ao, p. 188. In another manuscript, there is also a story about the rebels, saying that at the beginning of the rebellion, their members claimed to have magic power which could make a man's body invulnerable to swords with the help of the heavenly father and heavenly brother, but in reality they use strong alcohol mixed with some medicine. Before soldiers went to fight, their leader said a prayer, a chicken was killed and its blood was put in the alcohol. Each soldier drank a cup, and then they were so animated that they did not care for any danger. Ming-hsin Tao-jen, Fa-ni ch'u-chi 明心道人，髮逆初紀, quoted by Hsieh Hsing-yao in T'ai-p'ing T'ien-kuo ts'ung-shu shih-san-chung, t'se, 1, pp. 29-30. Were those records reliable, the Taipings may be said to be forerunners of the Boxers in 1900.

19. A letter to Yen Kuan-ch'a 閻觀察 [Yen Cheng-chi 承基] in Chung-fu-t'ang i-kao, 中復堂遺稿 (Block-print edition of 1867, ch. 5, pp. 9b-10.

20. Brine, p. 178.

21. Wolseley, Narrative of the War, p. 350.

22. T'ai-p'ing T'ien-kuo-shih k'ao-cheng-chi, pp. 42-55.

23. Ibid., p. 47, and Li Hsiu-ch'eng kung-tz'u, ch. 1, pp. 7-8.

24. Lo, pp. 52-54.

25. Fan Wen-lan, p. 43.

26. See Li Hsiu-ch'eng kung-tz'u, ch. 2, pp. 38-39.

27. The date of crushing the "Great Kiangnan Military Camp" was formerly given as May 5 or May 6, now Kuo T'ing-i ascertains it to be on May 6, 1860. See Kuo's Li-fa k'ao-cheng, p. 61. The reason of the victory was generally believed through hard fighting. Hsieh Hsing-yao discovered that there was not much fighting except that caused by a mutiny among the government troops because of the arrears of rations. Hsieh's T'ai-p'ing T'ien-kuo ts'ung-shu shih-san-chung, t'se I, part 2,

p. 19b. Other new light has been cast on the problem which is too small to interest the general reader.

28. See Ch'en's biography in the <u>Eminent Chinese</u>.

29. <u>T'ai-p'ing T'ien-kuo shih-shih lun-ts'ung</u>, p. 12.

30. <u>Chien-she yen-chiu</u>, 建設研究, vol. VIII, no. 6 (February 1943), pp. 27-33, also in <u>Chin-t'ien chih-yu</u>, pp. 208-220.

31. Yang Sung's article appears in the <u>Ch'ün-chung</u>, see note 16 of the same section.

32. For instance, the intellectual and brave leader, Lo Ta-kang who "once spoke to others, 'I joined the revolutionary army at the same time with Ch'in Jih-kang 秦日綱 and Hu I-huang 胡以晃 , and have rendered the same service, but because those two persons, who were old brethren of Kwangsi, were both made kings. I, being a native of Kwangtung, cannot get a marquis. There is nothing in the world which is so unfair as this. Does the Heavenly King forget that he himself is a native of Hua-hsien?' When Yang Hsiu-ch'ing heard of this, he dared not entrust Lo with important military duties." (<u>T'ai-p'ing T'ien-kuo yeh-shih</u>, ch. 15, p. 3). The good fighter Lai Wen-kuang, 賴汶光, was a cousin of Hung Hsiu-ch'üan's wife. Yang Hsiu-ch'ing was jealous of him and kept him away from military affairs. (<u>Ibid</u>., ch. 13, p. 31). In 1856 the Kwangtung faction joined hands with another minor Kwangsi faction led by Wei Ch'ang-hui to knock out Yang's faction. Wei then attempted to oppress the Kwangtung faction and finally he was killed. (Cf. Fan Wen-lan, p. 70) Li Hsiu-ch'eng, a native of Kwangsi, was not made Prince or King when other mediocre members of the Hung family were given such high honor until a document inviting Li to surrender to Manchu was intercepted by Hung. Then Hung made him "loyal prince." (<u>Li Hsiu-ch'eng kung-tz'u</u>, ch. 3, pp. 59-61).

33. See <u>Tsei-ch'ing hui-tsuan</u>, ch. 11, the items: "Lao-tsei," old bandits, and "Hsin tsei," new bandits.

34. <u>Li Hsiu-ch'eng kung-t'zu</u>, ch. 3, p. 62.

35. For instance, they liked red and yellow costumes while other people were forbidden to use such colors. The sedan chair of the Heavenly King was carried by sixty-four porters and that of the East King by forty, and the latter's retinue was usually from several hundred to one thousand. Whenever he went out, all people in the streets had to kneel down at the sides of the road where he passed. (See **Tsei-ch'ing hui-tsuan**, ch. 6, under three related items.)

36. Cf. Lo Erh-kang, <u>Hsiang-chün hsin-chih</u>, pp. 222-230, and <u>Shih-men ju-chiao-chi</u>, p. 53.

37. In 1859 Yung Wing made the following suggestions: "(1) to organize an army on scientific principles, (2) to establish a military school for the training of competent military officers, (3) to establish a naval school or a navy, (4) to organize a civil government with able and experienced men to act as advisers in the different departments of administration, (5) to establish a banking system, and to determine a standard of weight and measure, (6) to establish an educational system of graded schools for the people, making the Bible one of the textbooks, (7) to organize a system of industrial schools." (p. 109).

38. According to the account of a scholar captured by the Taipings, "Ku Ch'en, Hu-hsüeh huan-sheng chi", 顧琛，虎穴還生記, <u>Jen-wen</u>, 人文, vol. VI, no. 8 (October 1935), pp. 2-3, 7, and no. 9 (October 1935), pp. 10-13.

39. At the time of the rebellion there existed no working class in the modern sense of the word, which could have taken over the leadership of the rebellion. Although the Taiping T'ien-kuo controlled part of China, the Taiping peasant communism was utopian. Kara-Murza, p. 121.

VI. NEW LIGHT ON THE TAIPING RELIGION AND CALENDAR

1. "Chin Ko, Hung Hsiu-ch'üan tsung-chiao pien-i", 金革，洪秀全宗教辨疑, in <u>P'an-shih tsa-chih</u> 磐石雜誌, vol. II, no. 11 (November 1934), pp. 17-19. It is Hsieh Hsing-yao who says that the Taipings believe in Catholicism in an article in the <u>Pei-p'ing ch'en-</u>

pao, 北平晨報, and also in his T'ai-p'ing T'ien-kuo ti she-hui cheng-chih ssu-hsiang, p. 25. Chin's article also makes several mistakes, though his point that the Taipings are Protestants is correct per se.

2. This is a manuscript of a Ph. D. thesis of the History Department of Harvard University, 1946, 204 pp.

3. Such as Macfarlane, The Chinese Revolution, p. 146 and Chien Yu-wen, Shou-i-shih, p. 125, etc.

4. From the Old Testament there are five quotations from Genesis, chapters 1, 3, 4, 6, and 7; six quotations from Isaiah including two chapters and thirty-two verses; two from the Psalms, chapter 19 and verses 4-22 of chapter 33; one from Ecclesiastes, one verse only; and one from Jeremiah, fifteen verses. All together, eight chapters and fifty-three verses are quoted from the Old Testament. These are not very accurate "statistics" because there are a few places where the sentences seem to be quotations, but there is no indication of the source, and there are also one or two occasions where it is difficult to ascertain whether they are taken from the Old or the New Testament. Since the translation is very different from the English and later Chinese versions, it is not easy to identify passages.

5. Apparently there are few Chinese Taiping historians who have read and paid much attention to the Ch'üan-shih liang-yen, except for a casual reference. Hsieh and Lo speak little of this book; Chien made a brief resume of it which seems to be based on some English source like T. T. Meadows, and P'eng Tse-i gets the information about this book from Chien.

6. George Hunter McNeuv, Chinese First Preacher, Liang A-fa, (Shanghai 1934), p. 75.

7. See examples of unintelligible translations in section IV, note 87.

8. Mao I-heng's article in the Shen-pao Monthly, vol. 4, no. 1, (January 1935), pp. 169 ff., presents this idea very clearly.

9. "Several missionaries have visited them and have found their religious observances half Jewish and half Christian." See Macfarlane, p. 146. The main similarity to Judaism is the Taiping observance of the Sabbath on Saturday instead of Sunday, but now this charge is open to question, because their calendar is one day ahead of Western weekdays. The Western Sunday is the Taiping Saturday, and so on. See the next section.

10. "Hung was anti-Catholic and even slaughtered a Jesuit priest at Si-ka-wei", Brine, p. 351. See also Wolseley's observation translated by Chien Yu-wen in his T'ai-p'ing T'ien-kuo tsa-chi, p. 108.

11. See Brine, p. 287, where Hung tactfully refused the suggestion to allow the missionaries to preach Gospel in the interior. Nor did he like foreigners to teach Chinese the Bible, because "he thought the thing could be done by the Chinese themselves" (ibid., p. 286). Furthermore the Taipings required foreigners to be subject to their jurisdiction. (Alexander Michie, The Englishman in China during the Victorian Era, I, 380). "They were friendly, but they were not prepared to barter away their country's rights" (Cahill, p. 275). From these observations it is safe to say that the Taipings attempted to fight for national independence and international equality. Hung was a pioneer and harbinger of the modern nationalistic movement before Sun Yat-sen's enterprise.

12. Such as many quotations containing the term, "Shang-ti" from the Book of History, The Book of Odes, and Mencius, in the T'ien-ch'ing tao-li shu.

13. For instance: T'ien-fu shang-chu huang-shang-ti sheng-chih yüeh, "Tzu-ku ssu-sheng t'ien-pai-ting, na-yu yu-chi te-ch'eng-jen," 天父上主皇上帝聖旨曰，自古死生天排定，那有由己得成人，"From old death and life have been arranged and decided by Heaven, how could one follow oneself and become perfect?" T'ien-hsiung Yeh-su sheng-chih yüeh, "Ch'eng-jen pu-tzu-tsai, tzu-tsai pu ch'eng-jen," 天兄耶穌聖旨曰，成人不自在，自在不成人，"A perfect man is not free; a free man is not perfect." T'ien-wang chao-chih yüeh, "Shan-jen wu-ê yu-chi-lien, chen-hsin wu-chia wan-wan-

nien," 天王詔旨曰，善人無惡由己鍊，真心無
假萬萬年 ，"A good man without evil is refined by himself, a
sincere heart without hypocrisy lasts for myriads and myriads of years."
T'ien-ch'ing tao-li shu, p. 38.

14.   At first the Taiping funeral ceremony followed the Confucian
rites, allowing people to use a coffin and have a funeral parade.   Later
on all former practice was abolished and a coffin was not used, the corpse
was wrapped only in silk and satin.   Lo Erh-kang, "T'ai-p'ing T'ien-kuo
ching-chi k'ao," 太平天國經籍考 ，(A Study of Taiping publications), Hsüeh-yüan 學原 ，vol. II, no. 1 (1948).   After he committed
suicide, Hung's corpse was wrapped in the way described above.   See the
Diary of Tseng kuo-fan, t'se 20, the 6th moon, 28th, 1864.

15.   "The Confucian temples were spared, the state of Chekiang and
most of the thirteen ravaged provinces of China could best be described
in the words of Isaiah: 'Here cometh a troop of men; the city is fallen
and all the graven images of gods are broken to the ground.'"   Arthur
Moule, Half a Century in China, pp. 52-53.

16.   Cahill, p. 274.

17.   P. 284.

18.   A long note can be written if the correlated paragraphs, where
the ideas are summarized in the text, are translated in English.   To be
brief the sources are the T'ien-t'iao-shu (in T'ien-p'ing T'ien-kuo ts'ung-
shu, t'se 1), especially pp. 4-5; the Hsing-shih-wen (ibid., t'se 8),
especially pp. 7-8; Wang chang, tz'u-hsiung ch'in-mu, ch'in-erh kung-cheng
fu-yin shu (ibid., t'se 8), especially pp. 3b-5; and T'ai-p'ing T'ien-kuo
chao-chih.

19.   Shen-pao Monthly, vol. IV, no. 1, p. 17.

20.   When Shih Ta-k'ai was in Kwangsi, he met a Taoist or an Immortal
Chang T'ieh 張鐵 ，whose agnomen was Liao-k'ung, 了空 ，and who
boasted of having the power to swallow a knife and vomit fire.   Shih
treated him very politely, and gave him a chance to try his magic.   In
bare feet and unplaited hair, the Taoist held a sword in his right hand

and some charms in the left, recited spells, and then brandished a
sword everywhere with amazing bravery. <u>Hsin Chung-hua</u>, op. cit., vol. III,
no. 9, p. 72. See also note 18 of section V.

21. In <u>Li Hsiu-ch'eng kung-tz'u</u>, Hung Hsiu-ch'üan appears to be a
typical Taoist emperor. When state affairs were reported and instructions
were requested, Hung would digress from the point, or become angry saying
that God would take care of the Heavenly King, why should he worry about
it. When there was a shortage of food, and a request was made to accumulate
provisions to stand for a long siege of Nanking which he insisted be de-
fended, he would again become impatient and would dispose of the titanic
problem by saying "let people of the whole city eat sweat dew," by which
he meant "grass". (<u>Li Hsiu-ch'eng kung-tz'u</u>, ch. 2, p. 35b; ch. 3, pp. 52-
53, 57b, 62.) Hung found a good excuse for not attending public affairs.
"The Father descended in a dream and made a revelation to my wife, and
commanded that I should not attend to common things" (Brine, p. 294.)
It is not necessary to give sources for his well-known licentiousness and
harem. There is a good description of his palace in <u>Chung-ho Monthly</u>,
中和月刊 , vol. IV, no. 3 (March 1943), pp. 79-80.

22. As Hung Jen-kan says, "The Chief is a pious man, notwithstanding
all his errors, he devoutly worships God, and is a constant reader of the
Scriptures." (Lin-le, p. 294) M. T. Yeats and Brine both believe that
"whatever may be the opinions held with regard to the Taipings, their
creeds and their actions, there can be no doubt that their leader is
sincere in his own belief." (Brine, p. 63).

23. A fairly good article is written by Ch'en Hsün-t'zu 陳訓慈
to prove these points in detail and is published in the <u>Shih-hsüeh tsa-</u>
<u>chih</u> 史學雜誌 (compiled by the Chinese Historical Association,
Nanking) vol. I, no. 6 (December 1929), pp. 1-8, and vol. II, no. 1
(March 1930), pp. 1-2.

24. <u>Tseng Wen-cheng kung tsou-kao</u>, ch. 25, p. 29b.

25. See the "Cultural Objects Destroyed by the Taipings" in Hsieh
Hsing-yao, <u>T'ai-p'ing T'ien-kuo ts'ung-shu shih-san chung</u>, <u>t'se</u> I, pt. II,
p. 15b.

26. See Lo Erh-kang, <u>T'ai-p'ing T'ai-kuo shih k'ao-cheng chi</u>, pp. 97-114. Tung's essay gives a detailed explanation of the theory of the Taiping calendar.

27. Chien, <u>Shou-i-shih</u>, p. 260.

28. <u>T'ai-p'ing T'ien-kuo shih-shih lun-ts'ung</u>, p. 18.

29. <u>T'ai-p'ing T'ien-kuo li-fa k'ao-ting</u>, p. 32.

30. See note 26.

31. <u>K'ao-cheng chi</u>, p. 98, based on Hung Ta-ch'üan's statement.

32. <u>Ibid</u>., p. 115.

33. See The significance of the revolution of Taiping T'ien-kuo in <u>Shigaku Zasshi</u>, vol. XXIII, no. 7 (July 1912), pp. 780-783. The material is adopted in Ling Shan-ch'ing's <u>T'ai-p'ing T'ien-kuo yeh-shih</u>, ch. 6, pp. 1-6, Hsiao I-shan, <u>Ch'ing-tai t'ung-shih</u>, pt. II, vol. III, pp. 174-175, and Wang Chung-chi, <u>T'ai-p'ing T'ien-kuo ko-ming shih</u>, pp. 123-126.

34. First appears in <u>Shih-hsüeh nien-pao</u>, vol. II, no. 1 (September 1932). pp. 57-106, and then recollected in <u>T'ai-p'ing T'ien-kuo shih-shih lun-ts'ung</u>, pp. 14-117.

35. <u>K'ao-cheng chi</u>, p. 121.

36. The Title is <u>Chin-shih Chung-hsi shih-jih tui-chao piao</u>, 近世中西史日對照表 (The Commercial Press, 1936).

37. <u>K'ao-cheng chi</u>, p. 119.

38. <u>K'ao-cheng chi</u>, pp. 135, 137.

VII. NEW LIGHT ON TAIPING POLITICAL AND SOCIAL SYSTEMS

1. <u>T'ai-p'ing T'ien-kuo ti cheng-chih she-hui ssu-hsiang</u>, p. 4.

2. Shortly after the retarding of the revolution, such appellations as the Celestial King, Celestial Court, the Celestial Army, the Taiping T'ien-kuo, the new calendar, the Heir-Apparent or the Young Ruler, and the various generals were adopted. It is a mistake to consider that the Taipings did not establish a dynasty and adopt the reign title after they

took Yung-an. It is a mistaken belief, too, that Hung first used the title, T'ien-p'ing-wang, and later changed to T'ien-wang. See Chien, Shou-i-shih, pp. 207-08.

3. The biography of Hung Hsiu-ch'üan in the Ch'ing-shih kao, ch. 482, pp. 3b-5b, and Tsei-ch'ing hui-tsuan, ch. 3.

4. Ch'in-ting shih-chieh t'iao-li, pp. 6 8, and Ying-chieh kuei-chen, pp. 18-19.

5. Such as the Chao-shu kai-hsi pan-hsing lun, "On affixing the imperial seal on edicts and disseminating them" in T'ai-p'ing T'ien-kuo ts'ung-shu, t'se 4, in which there are twenty-five examination papers of poor quality. Even the theme does not make much sense, because the examinations were poorly made out and those who were examined were not well educated.

6. T'ien-ch'ao t'ien-mou chih-tu in T'ien-p'ing T'ien-kuo ts'ung-shu, t'se 1. The summary here given is only part of the contents.

7. Brine, pp. 249, 279.

8. Li Hsiu-ch'eng kung-tz'u, ch. 2, p. 34b.

9. Then followed by the Taiping date, the time limit, and the place to pay. The original document is in the Graduate School of National Peking University and reproduced in Lo Erh-kang's outline history, p. 90.

10. Li Hsiu-ch'eng kung-tz'u, ch. 2, p. 47. Note that, according to Li Hsiu-ch'eng, from time to time, capital money, seeds, and agricultural instruments were lent to people, to whom sometimes rice was distributed for the purposes of rehabilitation. See also ch. 2, pp. 27, 34b, 46b, and passim.

11. The Land Tax of the Yangtze Provinces before and after the Taiping Rebellion, Tsing-Hua hsüeh-pao, vol. X, no. 2 (April 1936), pp. 409-474.

12. Brine, p. 222.

13. Brine, p. 223

14. T'ai-p'ing T'ien-kuo shih-kang, pp. 90-96.

15. Hsieh Hsing-yao (T'ai-p'ing T'ien-kuo ts'ung-shu, t'se 1, pt. 2, p. 10), Fan Wen-lan and Chien Yu-wen all believe so.

16. Lin-le, p. 302.

17. L. H. Wheeler, The Foreigner in China (Chicago, 1881), p. 23.

18. "All marriage in the empire should not be arranged on terms of money" - T'ien-ch'ao t'ien-mou chih-tu, p. 3.

19. Lin-le, p. 317.

20. Ibid., p. 303; Chin-ling kuei-chia chi-shih lüeh (Hsieh Hsing-yao, T'ien-p'ing t'ien-kuo t'sung-shu, t'se 2), pp. 2, 3b, 4, 4b, 6b, 10, 11. Ch'ing-shih kao, ch. 482, p. 9.

21. Pp. 347, 348.

22. Chien Yu-wen, T'ai-p'ing T'ien-kuo tsa-chi, pp. 80, 121.

23. Pp. 106-107.

24. Chung-kuo cheng-chih ssu-hsiang-shih, pp. 307-315.

25. Lo, Hung Hsiu-ch'üan, pp. 49-51.

CHINESE CHARACTERS REFERRED TO IN THE TEXT

p. 1　曾國藩
　　　李秀成

p. 2　黃世仲, 洪秀全演義
　　　李昭壽
　　　凌善清
　　　程演生, 太平天國史料第一集
　　　劉復, 太平天國有趣文件十六種

p. 3　賊情彙纂
　　　張德堅
　　　謝興堯
　　　簡又文
　　　蕭一山
　　　太平天國叢書
　　　太平天國詔諭
　　　王重民
　　　太平天國官書補編
　　　俞大維
　　　羅邕
　　　沈祖基
　　　太平天國詩文鈔
　　　文獻叢編
　　　掌故叢編
　　　清實錄
　　　逸經

p. 4　太平天國雜記
　　　金田之遊及其他
　　　太平軍廣西首義史
　　　太平天國起義記

p. 5　太平天國史事論叢
　　　太平天國叢書十三種

p. 6　洪大全
　　　洪秀全
　　　金陵癸甲紀事略
　　　謝稼鶴
　　　粵逆陷寧始末記
　　　陳錫麒
　　　癸丑中州罹兵紀略
　　　陳善鈞
　　　庚申避亂實錄
　　　趙偉甫

p. 7　越州紀略
　　　儉德齋隨筆
　　　胡長齡
　　　長興
　　　干王洪仁玕等口供
　　　羅爾綱
　　　貴縣
　　　太平天國史綱

p. 8　太平天國叢考
　　　正中書局
　　　洪大全考
　　　朱九濤
　　　向榮
　　　洪秀全傳
　　　金田起義前洪秀全年譜
　　　天地會文獻錄
　　　湘軍新志
　　　綠營兵志

p. 9　太平天國史考證集
　　　董作賓

p. 10　郭廷以
　　　太平天國曆法考證
　　　太平天國史事日誌
　　　彭澤益, 太平天國革命思潮

p. 11　太平天國叢書
　　　非宇館文存
　　　太平天國革命運動

p. 12　范文瀾
　　　朱謙之
　　　梁岵廬

p. 13　梨本佑平
　　　佐野學
　　　外山軍次, 太平天國の上海
　　　清代籌辦夷務始末
　　　稻葉岩吉, 清朝全史
　　　但燾
　　　矢野仁一
　　　廣州府志
　　　野原四郎, 太平天國の亂
　　　世界歷史大系
　　　增井經夫